SP Freedom-Now Method

Be a happy non-smoker and stay a happy non-smoker

Sylvie Poudrette

SP Freedom-Now Method

© 2012 Sylvie Poudrette
All rights reserved

Publisher: Sylvie Poudrette
First Edition
Published: March 2012

ISBN: 978-0-9879902-0-4

Sales and distribution: Lulu.com
Printed by Lulu.com

Note for readers
Contents: Chapter nine starts at page 108 instead of page 107

To the memory of my parents,
Rachel and Lionel Poudrette

CONTENTS

INTRODUCTION 11
CHAPTER ONE 13
  SAYING GOOG-BYE TO CIGARETTES 13
    What is the smoker's pattern? 15
    Struggle with smoking 16
    What to expect when you stop smoking with this method: 17
    Different ways to stop smoking 18
    Making the decision 19
    Reasons for stopping smoking 22
    Tips 23
    Some people find it harder than others 24
    Why does the smoker want to smoke so much in the first place? 25
    Desire to quit smoking 27
    How to make it happen 27
    Begin to pay attention to your eating habits 27
    Desire and denial 27

CHAPTER TWO 29
  BENEFITS OF NOT SMOKING 29
    What to expect when you stop smoking: 29
    Focus and concentration 32
    What do I personally think about nicotine replacements? 34

CHAPTER THREE 37
  PLEASE HELP ME 37
  I AM AFRAID TO LOSE IT 37
    What are your fears about quitting smoking? 37
    Here are some fears you may encounter: 37
    Another way to look at it 39
    Don't be afraid to quit smoking 39

CHAPTER FOUR 43
  THE BIGGEST FEAR OF ALL: 43
  GAINING WEIGHT 43
    About weight gain 43

Other ex-smokers and I will tell you: 44
For those who have gained a lot of weight--eating habits:
.... 44
    Lack of nicotine 46
    Illusions 46
    Women and gaining weight 47
    Benefits of being fit 48

CHAPTER FIVE 49

  WHO AM I? 49
    Going through the addiction 49
    Going through the symptoms 49
    How to manage withdrawals symptoms: 52
    Other small issues 53
    Grieving 53
    Physical withdrawals 54
    Anger 55
    Depression 55
    Guilt 56
    Stress 57
    Influence of smokers 57
    Myths 58
    Once you are a non-smoker 60
    Ways of stopping smoking: 60
    The right time to quit smoking 62
    I don't really want to stop smoking—you know—social pressure 62
    What does it mean to me to be a non-smoker? 63

CHAPTER SIX 65

  TOOLBOX 65
    How to prepare the toolbox and use the tools: 65
    Tips: 70
    Here is an example of ritual: 71
    When it comes to quitting smoking, ... 73
    A word about cold turkey 75
    Reminders 75
    Relapses 77
    Create your ritual 78
    Relaxation and pleasure 79
    Good news about quitting 80

The last words on toolbox 82
What to do if nothing is working for you 83

CHAPTER SEVEN **85**

THE METHOD 85
What it is: 85
Personal Power 91
What does personal power mean to you? 91
Awareness 93
Focus and Concentration 93
Freedom 95
Joy 96
The Best of yourself—what it is? 97

CHAPTER EIGHT **101**

THE SELF-SUGGESTION PROGRAMS 101
How to practice your self-talk script 101

CHAPTER NINE **107**

SP FREEDOM-NOW METHOD 107
SELF-SUGGESTIONS PROGRAMS 107
First week 107
Program 1.1: Personal Power – Monday 107
Program 1.2: Awareness – Tuesday 108
Program 1.3: Focus and concentration – Wednesday . 109
Program 1.4: Freedom – Thursday 110
Program 1.5: Joy – Friday 111
Second week 112
Program 2.1: Personal Power – Monday 112
Program 2.2: Awareness – Tuesday 113
Program 2.3: Focus and concentration – Wednesday . 115
Program 2.4: Freedom – Thursday 116
Program 2.5: Joy – Friday 117
Third week 118
Program 3.1: Personal Power – Monday 118
Program 3.2: Awareness – Tuesday 119
Program 3.3: Focus and concentration – Wednesday . 120
Program 3.4: Freedom – Thursday 121
Program 3.5: Joy – Friday 123
Fourth week 124
Program 4.1: Personal Power – Monday 124

Program 4.2: Awareness – Tuesday 125
Program 4.3: Focus and concentration – Wednesday . 126
Program 4.4: Freedom – Thursday 127
Program 4.5: Joy – Friday 129
Bibliography 131
Websites 131

SP Freedom-Now Method

Be a happy non-smoker and stay a happy non-smoker

INTRODUCTION

This book is for the smoker who wants to quit smoking for good, and for the one who has tried before and failed many times. I have created a method that will motivate you to stay free from nicotine. In this method, you will not only find that it is possible to quit smoking for good but also be a happy non-smoker and stay a happy non-smoker.

Before getting any further, I would like to introduce myself shortly, and then the reason why I have written this book.

My name is Sylvie Poudrette. I was born in Drummondville, Quebec. My mother did not smoke but my father smoked for most of his life—he quit smoking when he was in his late fifties. Unfortunately, my mother passed away in 1971 from breast cancer and my father left us in April 2006 from prostate cancer. I have two sisters and one brother that are still smokers and two brothers that are on and off. I have started smoking at fifteen years old and quit at fifty. So for thirty-five years, I have smoked all my way up to end up very unhappy with myself.

I have tried seriously and sincerely to stop smoking for three years before quitting for good. Through these relapses, I have talked to people who had quit, and to those who have been like me: in hell, up and down. What I have learned from these three years of torture is that smokers deal with a very powerful drug; the one that does not leave marks or scars on your skin but makes you think that life is not worth living.

This nicotine addiction affects many aspects of smokers' lives. I am sure you have asked yourself like me this question before, "Why is it so hard to stop smoking in the first place?" After all, we all know that smokers are not stupid or little losers hoping to get lung cancer. Well, again I think the reason why it is so hard to quit is because smokers are dealing with a tricky addiction. This nicotine addiction makes you believe that it satisfies you at all levels all the time, then your mind and body keep you hooked on that belief and you keep smoking.

My method SP Freedom-Now will help you say good-bye to cigarettes in a natural way. I will use my smoker past to demonstrate how addicted I was to nicotine and how I found this method. As soon as I started using it, everything became easier. That was my first reward.

To me, this method has worked well because I have understood one thing about smoking: I enjoyed it when I smoked and now I enjoy it when I don't smoke. I had been a smoker for thirty-five years and NOW I have been FREE from nicotine since November 9, 2004. I do not feel like smoking—I do not want to smoke—people who are still smoking do not bother me anymore. I go everywhere I want and I feel free to be.

I call my method Freedom-Now because I believe that after this program, you will think like me, freedom now from nicotine is possible. Not only possible but feasible one day at a time while being a happy non-smoker. You do not believe me. You think that I am trying to fool you. I do not blame you, I was there before.

So let's begin. Enjoy the ride!

CHAPTER ONE

SAYING GOOG-BYE TO CIGARETTES

For most people, saying good-bye to cigarettes is not easy. However, thousands and thousands of smokers are doing just that every day. So it must be possible! For some, it is easier than for others. They are the lucky ones. But for those that find it very difficult, they are not alone. Nicotine is a strange and complicated addiction. It is not only legal but after consuming the substance, it does not do anything like alcohol or other chemical dependences would do immediately to the body. For instance, after smoking a cigarette, you do not look drunk or high with that funny attitude that could get you into trouble if you do not stop. No, on the contrary, right after a cigarette, you feel good and in control. Stimulated by the nicotine, you feel more in focus and motivated. Yet, after thirty minutes or so, you start to feel a little gnawing from inside. Nicotine is asking you to respond.

In the introduction, I said that I enjoyed it when I smoked and now I enjoy it when I do not smoke. What I mean here is that I responded differently to nicotine after a while. At the beginning, it is true that it was not easy to sweep away thirty-five years of smoking. Before finding this method and quitting for good, I went through an incessant three years of on and off. Pure torture! I wanted so much to stop smoking and yet, I kept on smoking. I knew I was deeply addicted. In those years, I became very annoyed by others who succeeded to be smoke-free. I often asked myself, "Why can't I stop smoking if I want so much to quit?" Really, I was pissed off by that one. Fortunately, I have learned a few things on my way to recovery.

You will certainly agree with the fact that smoking is not only hard on the body; it is hard on the wallet too. You have tried quitting smoking before and nothing has ever worked for you. You really wonder if you can do it. The only thing I can say is if I did it you can too.

I have developed this method for stopping smoking because I believe there is an easier way of quitting smoking without suffering too much. So in order to put this method together, I have done lots of research on the subject. In those three years of wanting so much to stop smoking, I have checked everything I could on the market, talked to people who had stopped and tried different methods, etc. After all that, I created the SP Freedom-Now Method. I now can say that I am a happy non-smoker and you can too if you want to. It is easy when your desire and decision work together. I know you are sceptic. You do not even like to hear or read it when I say it. Well, keep reading—you will be surprised.

I believe that this method will help you stop smoking and give you the motivation to remain a non-smoker. If you have smoked for years like I did, your habit is deeply ingrained in you. Your mind is programmed as a smoker, and in order to reach the mind you will have to be first in the here and now and use your personal power. When you stop smoking, the brain plays dirty tricks on you. It needs its fix. It is ready to lure you into its traps by any means. By being more and more aware of it, you will be better prepared. How? By telling the mind what to do. The most effective way I found to reach the brain is by using self-suggestions—real—down to earth—uplifting self-suggestions. Like I said, I have tried everything before. So the only way I was capable of telling the mind what to do without losing too many feathers was first, being in the cold turkey mode (feather and turkey go well together), and second, using a natural self-suggestions program in the morning. We will talk about it later on.

For those who are using nicotine replacements or have any health concerns please see your doctor first. He is the only one that can answer all issues related to your health and mind, and refer you to the right person if necessary.

Important: in that book, I will not talk too much about the bad effects of tobacco on your health. Many people have already done a good job on that. But if you feel that you need it to help you quit, read the literature on this addiction or go see on line all the websites talking about the dangers of tobacco. In fact, there are thousands and thousands of people thinking that scaring you is the best way to make you stop. In my case, it made me smoke more than before, so that was not a good thing. **The smoker does not like when you tell him what to do. You see it is part of the smoker's pattern.**

What is the smoker's pattern?

For most of the smokers, a certain pattern establishes itself quickly at the beginning—after getting hooked on nicotine on the first cigarettes; they ignore the obvious dangers of smoking, and then just keep on doing it. Later on, this pattern becomes for them a whole smoking lifestyle.

It is also true that smokers do smoke for different reasons at different periods of life. Some do so to ease stress or loneliness, others to prevent weight gain or for self-image. But the one thing they share is they are all addicted to nicotine.

To me, smoking is not only an addiction—it is an act of rebellion about everything the smoker secretly or openly disagrees with.

Some smokers are so addicted to nicotine that they think everyone wakes up in the morning with a cigarette. After smoking, they start waking up and feel human again. And then once they are well awake, they feel they need cigarettes to give them energy to make it through the day. If they are under stress and nervous, the cigarette calms them down—if they do a good job, the cigarette becomes the reward. So giving up this wonder drug seems ludicrous to them.

However, as soon as they go out, it is another story. If they dare smoking in the street, people look at them. If they go visit people that do not smoke, they are the ones of the few smokers that do it outside. Social pressures are everywhere, and smokers start feeling trapped, they really feel that they are living in jail. The game is not funny anymore, and they are right.

Struggle with smoking

I have experienced in the past the struggle with smoking and the agony associated with the habit. When I was in a stressful situation, I was a compulsive smoker—could not stop. A chain smoker. In my addictive mind, I thought it was helping me think faster about a solution to the situation I was facing. That was part true; I was really stimulated by the nicotine because I made my mind believe with the time that responding to stress by smoking was part of the solution. However, I now know that it was just an illusion of the mind.

This method will help you believe that you do not need to smoke anymore to face stressful situations. In the introduction to SP Freedom-Now Method, I said, "In this method, you will not only find that it is possible to quit smoking for good but also be a happy non-smoker and stay a happy non-smoker." You think that I am full of...I am happy to say that I was before but I am not anymore since I have stopped smoking. I hope you have a good sense of humour—if not, this book is not for you. On your first days with this method, you will hate me with all your heart. Please do. Some of you will cry a lot for no reasons at the beginning before having some fun in life. But let me assure you that you will begin to enjoy life more and more after quitting. You will feel better more often and for longer periods of time, and then you will simply feel better for no particular reason.

What to expect when you stop smoking with this method:
- You will be more aware of what you are doing.
- You will know if you kid yourself.
- You will learn how to let off steam—to unwind.
- You will learn how to use your practical wisdom and manage the fears related with stopping smoking.
- You will be more in touch with the Best of yourself.
- You will live more in harmony with yourself and make the best of what you have one day at a time.

- You will experience more often to be in the "here and now".
- You will simply enjoy life more.
- For those who have children, you will give a good example. You will walk the talk.

Struggling with nicotine is not funny. There are so many ups and downs along the road, you really wonder if you can make it. Your story is my story. I have been there. I know it is hard. But you can make it because I did. I know what I am talking about. I know all the little dirty secrets of smoking. Sure, it is a drug difficult to kick out but if you kick it where I think you will, you will be on the road of freedom.

For those who have already stopped smoking, congratulations! Just read through the book. It will encourage you to stay a non-smoker. It takes a lot of courage to make the decision of quitting and stick with it. However, once you have made the decision, the desire takes over and supports you in your actions. For the smokers who really want to quit, I would ask you to help yourselves by starting reducing your intake tomorrow morning. And each time you smoke—**DO JUST THAT**—do not do anything else. Sit down, relax and smoke your cigarette. Pay attention to your smoking from the first puff to the last one. Enjoy.

Different ways to stop smoking

Let me introduce you to different ways to stop smoking. There are many stop smoking aids on the market, just to name any: the nicotine patch, the nicotine gum, herbs, inhalers and nasal sprays. There are books, tapes and CDs about stopping smoking. And then, there are other methods like hypnotherapy, acupuncture, etc.

I have tried many of these methods. And for three years, I have tried and failed, tried and failed and again and again and again. I was very unhappy about that. One day, I made up my mind—I decided that I wanted to laugh before dying. I was determined to try everything to make it happen. The first thing I did was to stay away from people who dramatize everything. It was indeed a good decision because my quality of life improved immediately.

Making the decision

The day I made the decision I would be the boss of my life and not the smoke; I became aware of lots of little things. My awareness showed me that my life was organized around my smoking habits and that, for the past thirty-five years. As you know, before quitting for good, I have tried everything for three years—nonstop: the patch (3 months) then the nicotine gum (2 months)—start smoking again for a short period. Stop again with another kind of patches, then nicotine gums again, then cold turkey (no more than 3 days) then start smoking again, then stop and use again these aids. After using these nicotine replacements for a year, I could see through walls. I had vivid and stupid dreams. I was very nervous and restless. I could not sleep. I had complete lack of focus and concentration—and a very low level of awareness. I was always tired. I was depressed. I worked less and less. I had no more motivation to write or do other work. When I was home, I had to take short naps to go through the day—sometimes, I cried for no reasons. I gained weight fast when I stopped smoking. I lost weight fast when I started smoking. The ups and downs took its toll on me. I became very depressed and moody. **To sum up all of that, to me life was not worth living anymore.** So I would start smoking again but this time for longer periods of time. After a while, I would be fed up and stop again.

In the third year, I still wanted to stop smoking but this time for good. I was ready to try again everything. I used my willpower to stop smoking—however, it did not take long before I started envying everyone who was smoking or hating them for the same reason. The weirdest method I have ever tried was invented by a French man from France, a naturopath, his name I want to forget forever. Someone that I know had stopped smoking using this method some years before. As I was determined to quit no matter what, I asked that person if I could use it. As she was and still is a very nice person, she sent me the kit by mail. With that method, morning and night, I had to listen to a relaxation tape—everything was fine with that. But then during the day, each time I smoked a cigarette, I had to put a plastic filter on my cigarette filter and listened at the same time with the help of earphones to a strange cosmic noise coming from hell. In his introduction, this man was telling you to reduce your smoking each day which I did. However, days after, I started smoking more and more, and I sent back the package to the person. I just said it did not work for me. I did not want to insult her. It worked for her. What can I say? After it, I did read books on quitting smoking but they were too scary for me. Most of them were based on: you quit or you die.

Then, I began reading about different spiritual approaches to stop smoking, but that was too high in the sky for me. What I needed was a down to earth method that would help me to be aware of my bad habit. For those interested on this subject, the Buddhism Tradition and Zen are the best ones I can think of. They talk about awareness and be in the present moment. I also read books about personal power, awareness and freedom from addictions. However, I did not want to go through meditation and do the exercises of being in the "here and now" to stop smoking. To me, these things were again a never-ending job. I needed something faster that would help me focus on what I was doing. Something that would make me aware of what was going on in me and around me. Finally, something that I could remember during the day. I began to write kind of affirmations—then, they became self-suggestions. I call them self-suggestions because they are phrased in a certain way and are telling you why you are doing that. I wrote some on personal power, awareness, focus and concentration, freedom and joy. Then, I started reading them in the morning.

 Here, it is important to mention that I did read them even if I was smoking a few cigarettes a day. A strange thing happened after repeating them a few days—I started being more aware of what I was doing. One morning—out of the blue—I said to myself firmly, "The best time to stop smoking is NOW." And I did it cold turkey. The first four days were difficult but a way easier after. Encouraged, I kept reading aloud these self-suggestions to myself in the morning. The first month, I had my ups and downs but less intense than when I was on the patch or the gum. So to me, that was a very good motivator, and then the second month, I had more good days than bad days. I really started enjoying doing my program in the morning. It seemed to help me to go through the day while reminding me why I was doing it. My motivation began being stronger than my addiction. That was good news to me. And it is now good news to you.

 Before doing these self-suggestions, I told you that I used my willpower for stopping smoking. It did not work at all for me. To those of you who believe that you will be able to stop smoking with your willpower, I have bad news for you. After asking people that have stopped smoking for many years and proud to say that they have done so with their willpower—I have discovered that they still miss the feeling of smoking. I like to call them the "willpow-pow non-smokers". If they are in a party and see people smoking, most of the "willpow-pow non-smokers" will envy the smokers while relying on their willpower to retain their anger and rage. You see, they are still unhappy because their feelings always resurface in the face of the smoke. If you observe them longer, you may find that they have replaced the nicotine addiction by another one. Anyway, I let you judge of that.

It does not mean that the smoke does not bother me when I am in an area full of smoke but I do not care if people smoke or do not smoke anymore. If I cannot take that smoky atmosphere, I just get out of there. Period.

The second important thing after making a decision about quitting smoking is **being prepared.**

For those who are still smoking a lot, each time you smoke—do just that. Be aware of each puff you inhale. Say "bye-bye" to the cigarette in your mind. Do it each time you smoke. You will feel a little silly at the beginning but you will see how awareness works.

Moreover, if you create your own ritual, you will be more mentally prepared to deal with overeating, mild depression, mood swings, crankiness and other negative behaviours. I will talk about it in other chapters.

Reasons for stopping smoking

Just before making your list of reasons for stopping smoking, I will ask you, "Do you remember the first time you started smoking?" "Did you feel like a grown up?"

Write it down in a few sentences—other memories will come up with that.

In my case, I started smoking secretly and partially at fifteen, and then regularly at sixteen. In fact, I did it officially the day my mother died. My father did not like it but could not say too much—he was himself a heavy smoker. In that earlier period, I simply wanted to identify myself with people who smoked—at school or at parties. To me, they looked cool, adventurous and less fearful; I wanted that. But after a short while I started enjoying it and bang! I was hooked.

Tips

I will go through some tips right away and I will repeat them in a more structured way later on.

- **First thing first:** write down to yourself ten reasons for wanting to stop smoking. It can be anything you don't like about smoking. Then, rewrite it by priorities. Put this list somewhere where you can see it when you walk by in your house or bring it with you. Whatever works for you.
- Choose a date when you know you can relax at home the first two days.
- As soon as you wake up in the morning, drink at least two glasses of water in a row—thirsty or not.
- During the day, drink lots of water or juice or else—six to eight glasses a day.
- Be aware of each time a craving occurs: stop everything if possible. Think about the trigger behind it. Tell yourself it will pass in a few seconds. If you want to cry—cry.
- If you feel dizzy and miserable, take a short nap. The first week, whenever you have a chance, lie down. For example, lie down just

the time you would usually smoke that cigarette. Get up right away if you feel restless and move.
- When you feel highly irritated, annoyed or mad, have a walk or work out, or put on some rock' and roll music and dance your heart out.
- Chewing sugarless gum can help a lot at the beginning. However, as soon as it becomes too hard on your teeth usually after thirty minutes—get rid of it. Replace it with another one if you still feel like chewing.
- Candies for a short while can help too. In fact, anything can help. Be creative.

Some people find it harder than others

Like I said, I have tried stopping smoking for three years—on and off. I was a nicotine junkie. Each time, I quit smoking it felt like I did not enjoy life anymore. Some days, I just wanted to die. And when I would start smoking again, all these morbid thoughts would leave me by magic. I could not understand it. So needless to say that I was very resistant to giving up cigarettes even if I wanted.

Everyone knows some smokers that have or had heart attacks, lung cancer, and emphysema (disease of the lungs in which the air sacs become distended and lose elasticity). People that have never smoked in their lives are more than surprised when they see these convalescents coming back from the hospital, still smoking. To them, the first question that comes to mind is why? To me, the only way I can understand it is probably for the same reason mentioned earlier—life is not enjoyable anymore without smoking. It is not worth living. Some of them think that if they cannot smoke anymore, they prefer to disappear from the face of the earth. Some experts and other ex-drugs addicts say that kicking the nicotine addiction is harder than cocaine or heroin addiction.

It is not funny to be miserable. You now understand that the desire to quit smoking has to be backed up by the desire to live. Smokers have to convince their mind and body that there are just advantages to quit smoking. How the hell do they do that? By reprogramming themselves with a new way of looking at life. **Another warning here: for those who suffer from panic attacks, severe anxiety, stress, etc. Please, see your doctor first.**

People who have succeeded to quit for good will tell you that there are just benefits. Period. They feel more relaxed and healthier—they have a stronger immune system that gives them a higher quality of life. They live longer.

Here are some reasons why people have stopped smoking:
- To give up deadly health risks.
- To gain control over the powerless feelings of having an addiction.
- To save money.
- To protect others from second hand smoke.
- To remove social pressures.
- To breathe more easily and stop coughing.
- To smell better to others

Why does the smoker want to smoke so much in the first place?

We have seen in the smoker's pattern that this one starts smoking at a relatively young age. Once addicted, he enjoys nicotine more and more. He always finds reasons for smoking. Each time he lights up, a wonderful feeling of satisfaction invades his body. Then he thinks that smoking helps him get through the day. It is one of his ways of dealing with life. Nicotine makes him happy when he wants to feel happy, and then if he wants to add some melancholic or poignant or emotional moments to his life, nicotine will do so for him. For some, smoking gives them an image, a kind of aura of mystery. These images seen in movies or ads affect the smoker one way or the other. Sometimes, in a glamorous way; others times in an addicted way. Whatever suits his mood! Image, image, image. When you are young, it counts. If you don't smoke, there is a risk of not being accepted by the gang. Or the images of your heroes seem so powerful when they smoke that you just want to emulate them. Hey! At least, smoking is something you can do to look like them.

When I was young, smoking was my rebel thing to do. Each time, I saw a movie with a rebel who smoked—it just reinforced my urge for smoking. I do remember that many of those rebels on the big screen were chain smokers that could succeed to do all kinds of stunts while smoking. They were my heroes and heroines. They were in total control of the situation. I liked that. I even became good at juggling things while smoking too. Multi-tasking and smoking at the same time were one of my specialties. Now, when I think about it, I laugh at it; it was so ludicrous. I believe that many people do smoke to prove something, or to be accepted, or to fit in or just to annoy others.

So if you really want to quit, you really need to like yourself enough to do it. One of the best reasons to quit smoking is YOU. For those who want to give up for others, it will work for a while but you might become resentful. You will try to stay motivated but will be misguided on the road of freedom. Others can motivate you enough at the beginning to stop smoking but if the pressure is too strong, they can present a trap for the addicted.

Desire to quit smoking

The desire to stop smoking has to be genuine and articulated in a way that will be effective in the long term. There is a big difference between thinking and saying—saying and doing. It is better to say, "I want to give up smoking" than "I think I should stop smoking."

How to make it happen

Pretend often that you are a non-smoker. Act as one and be in the moment. Play it in your make-believe world. Ask yourself, "What would I do with my empty hands when I sit down or when I read or am on the phone? Start doing it.

Begin to pay attention to your eating habits

Lots of failures are associated with the fear of gaining weight, particularly for women. They use it as an excuse for maintaining the habit—been there, done it—they fear they will put on weight should they give up smoking. I will come back to it in another chapter.

Desire and denial

You understand that the desire to give up smoking must be stronger than the one to continue if you want it a success. But in order to think this way, you have to be motivated. The main reason for wanting to give up smoking is usually health—that means feeling good. With all the information available everywhere, the smoker cannot fool himself anymore into thinking that smoking will not harm him if he continues. There is too much evidence to the contrary.

You think it will be easier to make up your mind about quitting smoking if you read all the negative stuff. But even if you know for sure that smoking tastes awful, costs a fortune and kills, it will not be enough. In my case, I was still doing it even if I knew better because I was in denial—you see, in the first attempts to stop smoking, I felt deprived and sick. But once I stopped for good, I realized just how nice it was to be free.

When I think about all those years of puffing, I recognize that I put myself in jail. I sentenced myself to a lifetime of bad breath, stained teeth, yellow fingers, burnt clothes, smelly hair. My house and clothes smelled the old tobacco. It was a never-ending life of slavery. As soon as I understood the illusion of smoke, the reasons for smoking disappear into thin air. Suddenly, I was the magician. It worked for me because I knew all the tricks that nicotine addiction play on the person.

You too, you can be the magician if you want to. In this book, you will learn how to prepare yourself properly. You will get all the necessary tools in your magic box to perform the act. And then you will see that the more you practice, the better you do it with confidence and grace.

CHAPTER TWO

BENEFITS OF NOT SMOKING

What to expect when you stop smoking:
At all levels, it will be different. It will actually be more pleasant. Do not worry—you will come back to the things you like to do, and you will be surprised to feel how peaceful not smoking is.

In the morning, you will feel more energetic, more conscious, alert and aware. Enjoying yourself here and now will be your new way of life. The magic of now will empower you through ups and downs, smooth sailings and bumpy rides. Whatever it is, you will not reach anymore for a cigarette to deal with these events. You will reach rather for your personal power and awareness of the moment to deal with them.

Once you are free from nicotine, you start living fully your life. You walk up stairs without coughing or become out of breath—you enjoy again the delicious taste and smell of food—you spend your money on things you desire—and you reward yourself the way you want. In my case, I chose to work less and do things I enjoy like writing this book, writing fiction, screenwriting and so on. Spending time on what I like to do is a benefit and a big reward to me.

The number one benefit non-smokers enjoy the most is being free. Here, freedom has no price. They have regained control of their lives over nicotine. For parents, it could mean giving a good example to their children—they walk the talk. For others, enjoying more time with family, friends and children without going out every thirty minutes or so to smoke is a big accomplishment.

There are so many other benefits to it. I will add some more all along the book. If you want to enjoy all the benefits of not smoking, this SP Freedom-Now Method will show you how to do just that.

With this method you are so aware of each moment that it becomes easier to make a decision and harder to deceive yourself. Once you start it, the self-suggestions back you up in your choices and you feel better faster.

But before doing it, we have to look closely at this addiction. Do you remember how embarrassing it is to always be the big stinker on the elevator or the bus? Have you asked yourself why some smokers fully aware that smoking is killing them continue to smoke anyway? I have mentioned some of the reasons for it in the chapter before. Here is another angle to look at it. The smoker adopts a lifestyle where cigarettes are so tied to it that he thinks that if he quits smoking, he will not be able to keep going from the morning to the evening. He seriously thinks he will always experience the painful withdrawal symptoms, and this is a nightmare to him. Somewhere in the smoker's mind, the fear of quitting smoking becomes greater than the fear of dying from smoke. This is the effect of nicotine addiction. In other chapters, you will see that fears and illusions are behind this strange and weird thinking.

Luckily, the ex-smoker will tell you that there is life after smoking and withdrawals do not last forever. After quitting smoking, you will be pleasantly surprised to find out that you are able to cope with life more efficiently than when you were a smoker because you already feel better about yourself. You will feel well rested and refreshed when you wake up in the morning. In general, you will be calmer than when you smoked. And here, something important to mention—even under stress, you will not experience the panic reactions you used to feel whenever your nicotine fell below acceptable level.

You will also realize that you do not need a cigarette to give you a boost of energy. This is a myth: you will not live a life of withdrawals. These symptoms peak within three days—you will probably feel uncomfortable for three weeks but it will be tolerable.

And then, you will find that your life will become simpler, happier, cleaner and most importantly healthier than when you were a smoker.

About failure now. Don't forget that if you fail—IT IS NOT A BIG DEAL. Relapse is part of the deal. All right! However, relapse has a tendency to make you feel miserable. It is time to engage a conversation with yourself when you smoke; it could sound something like this, "My cigarette my friend—you stink, I stink. You control me totally. When you say, "Jump". I jump. I have enough. So now, it's time to say good-bye to you."

This SP Freedom-Now method will often remind you to live in the present moment. We will see that the self-suggestion programs talk more about the—here and now—than the nicotine addiction itself. Why? Because this way, you will be more motivated to do them. And after a little while, you will enjoy replacing your old addiction by a new one—freedom. This is the best gift you can give yourself. You will appreciate more to be alive and feel lighter when you pay attention to the moment. Feeling to the max is wonderful. It is a moment of conscious appreciation for getting another chance, another day. This brings us to another benefit.

Focus and concentration

This method will also help you focus and concentrate. You will learn to focus on what is here and now. You will enjoy your capacity for change, and your clear ability to manifest it. And every day that you manage to meet your goals and achieve things for yourself, it will be a cause for celebration.

The self-suggestion programs are designed to help you focus better by reminding you to take deep breaths when needed. This in turn will cleanse your system, relieve immediate cravings and relax your body. Breathing with awareness will support your best effort by focusing your intention on the moment. In fact, you will be your best observer and best friend. You will become more aware of your feelings and emotions; you will understand more deeply your habits patterns and consequently, enhance your effectiveness in your life.

When you stop smoking, you realize that you have developed a strong habit to put something in your mouth. Try to find food that is healthy for you—especially crunching or crackling food like carrots, celery, apples, etc. Some people use toothpicks. For those who like chewing gums, choose sugarless gum. In my case, chewing gum helped me through the two addictions, smoking and overeating. But eating more at the beginning is very normal.

However, it becomes a problem when after the third month, you cannot stop eating. You know you have to do something but you cannot put your mind into working it out. For those who hate exercising, I have a fun way to get rid of those extra pounds—I dance them around. Put some energetic music on and dance your heart out. In my case, rock' and roll music seems to do the job better than others. Remember you are creating a new you, a person who is not afraid anymore of its emotions, and knows how to express them appropriately. When your old feelings or memories resurface, take it like an opportunity to clear out anything that was not dealt with—and this as often as needed.

Your focus and attention will support you through times of change and uncertainty. When you feel insecure and anxious, it will be time to remind yourself to live one day at a time. Some days will be better than others—this is the way life is. However, when you do your self-suggestions on a regular basis in the first months, you will have more good days than bad. Just for that, it is worth it. Sometimes, I still do my self-suggestion programs just for the fun of it. To me, it is a good starter for the day.

The benefits of using the SP Freedom-Now Method are interesting. First, the non-smoker has the satisfaction of knowing that every morning during the week, he has done his homework by reading aloud these statements for twenty minutes or so rather than using nicotine replacements. When you work at it—it works. Second, these statements remind the non-smoker to live in the present which in turn enhance his self-confidence and self-esteem. If at any time in the future, he is tempted to start smoking again, he can use the same technique to stop again, often in a very short period.

And one day at a time, you will see that the benefits of non-smoking are greater than smoking.

You will not be able to lie to yourself anymore.

To me, quitting smoking is one of the greatest things I have accomplished in my life. I have never felt as good as that! Every happy non-smoker will tell you that quitting smoking was the best thing ever they did for themselves.

With this method, somewhere in your mind, you begin understanding that you cannot go back anymore to that grey world. You realize that smoking is an addiction and a bad habit. And this time you do not feel like smoking because it does not make sense anymore to you.

In your new world, you completely understand that you give up nothing but an illusion. So nothing is nothing. You now know without a doubt that smoking is stupid because it does not change anything in your life.

What do I personally think about nicotine replacements?

After using nicotine patches and nicotine gums on and off for three years, I personally think that they are just good to prolong the chemical and mental addiction.

However, I have to be fair. It helped me to get used to not having a cigarette between my fingers or in my mouth but other than that, it was the same misery when I stopped using them—no more nicotine. I started smoking again because the cravings are always in the background waiting to get you. In those three years, I did not stop spending money in order to find the right thing for me. With the time, I became very discouraged and even depressed. It seemed that nothing was working.

During that same period, a dear friend of mine became sick, he had lung cancer. Like me, he was off and on. We often shared with each other how miserable we were. My friend tried his best. He had some relapses.

Then one day, after using this method, I succeeded to quit smoking for good. On his side, my friend stopped smoking too but unfortunately his health deteriorated quickly—his lung cancer was too advanced. He passed away June 2, 2005. I had a very though time to deal with his loss but I did not smoke. I did not have the desire to. Nothing. I knew that was it.

CHAPTER THREE
PLEASE HELP ME I AM AFRAID TO LOSE IT

What are your fears about quitting smoking?
Many smokers will not answer the question directly—instead, they will make a kind of statement like, "the cigarette is a good friend. I can always count on it when I need it. Quitting is like losing a good friend."

I will reply, "Yes, you are right. Yet, this so-called friend will stab you in the back with the time."

Here are some fears you may encounter:
- Fear of not being able to cope with people around you— for example: what would you do if your spouse, partner, lover is a smoker? Like the song, "Should I stay or should I go?" I must admit this is a touchy one here but I believe your awareness and wisdom will tell you what to do. If it does not bother you, you know what to do. If it does, well you know what is coming up! Seriously now, we all know couples in which one of the partners does smoke. And it works for them. So! It is always up to you.
- Fear of gaining weight. * There is a complete chapter on this issue. (Chapter Four)

- Fear of failure. Nobody likes to fail.
- Fear of pain—of suffering. Life is not always the way we want but if you stay with the pain that withdrawals bring long enough—it will go away faster when you have another attack of cravings. Especially, if you are aware only of the pain when you have it. A good way to deal with it is each time a craving occurs and you start feeling very uncomfortable, say to yourself, "It's hard now but I know tomorrow, it will be twice easier."
- Fear of giving up your crutch or pleasure.
- Fear of not enjoying life anymore.
- Fear of not being able to handle stress.
- Fear of going through an awful trauma to get free.
- Fear of never being completely free from the craving.

So, each time you put all your attention on each puff while smoking, you will slowly remove these fears because you can articulate them now. You cannot hide them anymore.

Like the pills poppers, smokers are drug addicts. This is all they are; no more no less. If you accept it for what it is, you awareness will clarify a lot of things about yourself and your fears. This SP Freedom-Now method will support you when you need it. You will see that your awareness and desire to quit are stronger than your fears because it comes from deep inside. It is easier to succeed when you totally agree with what you are doing. After all, this is the reason I have written this book and this is the reason you are reading it right now—**quitting smoking for good without losing it**.

Another way to look at it

Smokers are smart. I mean smart drug addicts. They know smoking is bad for them. They are well informed about the bad press: poor health, less money in the pocket, stigma associated to smoking, etc. Yet, they continue to smoke in spite of that. Why? Again it is because their fears keep them hooked.

It takes courage to quit smoking but with awareness and time on your side, your nicotine withdrawals will be less and less intense and noticeable. Your fears will do the same. Intense desire is the enemy of fear. When you are more fed up than afraid, you take action toward your goal.

Don't be afraid to quit smoking

If you constantly worry about weight gain and failure, it will drain all your energy, make you feel bad and paralyze your actions

So a good way to quit smoking is doing it one day at a time. The expression "one day at a time" is a wonderful and wise way of thinking and doing things in life. So break through your fears and quit smoking just for today. Say to yourself in the morning, "Today I won't smoke—just for today. Tomorrow, I don't know but today I won't smoke—just for today."

Earlier I said, "Be aware of your discomfort when you are feeling one." I know it not always possible for you to stop everything and be aware of your discomfort. Ex: at work, if you are in the middle of something or simply under pressure or dealing with people—just let it be. This is life. However, whenever you have a chance—DO IT. Stop everything. Pay attention only to your pain. WHY? Because you will experience less and less suffering with the time. Here, I mean physical and emotional suffering due to nicotine removal.

Each time you feel sad, lonely, angry, envious, resentful, look at these emotional pains as the drama of life. We all have that. Your mind and body will tell you that smoking helps you deal with it. However, if you let your awareness working through it long enough—it will tell you that smoking has nothing to do with these feelings. You have them with or without smoking. This is the truth and reality of life.

For those who have stopped smoking. Once again, congratulations. However, keep reading. You will probably learn something new about this addiction that will remind you how wonderful it is to be a non-smoker. For those who still smoke—just remember: each time you smoke a cigarette—do just that. Look at the smoke—smell it, taste it, and say to your friend the cigarette, "Bye-bye" I know it sounds silly but you will be surprised what it does after a while.

For those who went through many relapses, take heart! Quitting smoking is hard. It is hard because you have not found the right way to do it yet. With this method, you will learn why it did not work before and why it will work now. One of the reasons it will work is simply because now you know what you are doing and why you are doing it.

Failure is no fun. Been there. Each time that you start at square one, it makes you a little depressed. Your self-esteem drops down and then, you say to yourself, "I can't do anything; I am such a failure—or I'll never be able to quit."

In my case, hidden somewhere in my mind, my biggest fear was quitting smoking for life. This lifetime decision scared me to death. But again, the addiction was playing with me, trying to convince me that I was not able to do that—I was too weak—I had no personal power. When you quit smoking, your mind plays tricks on you all the time and tries to sabotage your best efforts. Let's say, you need all your mind to face a dateline. You think five things at the same time or you come up with nothing. Your addicted brain will try to make you believe that you need to smoke in order to concentrate, to be inspired or to be creative, etc.

If you relapse, try again to stop until it becomes a habit. For example, say to yourself, "I won't smoke this morning—just this morning. This afternoon—just this afternoon. This evening—just this evening."

And as soon as you get stronger again, do it only "one day at a time." You will see that it is a good way to go through difficulties.

I know that you already know that. However, this time—stop thinking it and live it! And you will see that day after day—will become months. And after a year, you will be laughing at how easy it was.

CHAPTER FOUR

THE BIGGEST FEAR OF ALL: GAINING WEIGHT

About weight gain
- Please see you doctor and read all you can about the problem of food addiction if you feel that you may have an overeating habit.

When I gave up smoking for good, I gained fifteen pounds at the beginning. However, I lost ten pounds within that year. And now, I weigh the same as before. So, I agree with the fact that you may put on weight because you are so used to doing something with your hands and mouth that you tend to substitute snacks for cigarettes. Do not worry; if you eat more at the beginning, it is normal. The body will become accustomed to its new free-smoke habit, and it will adjust itself accordingly. But if you eat and eat and eat after the third month, it means to me that you are moving the problem (smoking) instead of getting rid of it. Reach for help if you have a challenging time with overeating. And do not forget that you have already accomplished something great, so now you can work on this issue too "one day at a time."

Put yourself together and celebrate your freedom from nicotine. The self-suggestion programs can uplift you when you feel low.

Look often at yourself in the mirror, particularly after a shower or a bath—you will see that you cannot fool yourself anymore. Now you understand that everything you do, you do it for you. A smoke will not solve the overeating problem. Ask other ex-smokers. There are so many things you can now enjoy.

Other ex-smokers and I will tell you:
- Yes, you can survive without a cigarette.
- Yes, you can enjoy life without a cigarette.
- Yes, you can appreciate a good meal without a cigarette.
- Yes, you can have a drink without a cigarette.
- Do not put yourself in stressful situations during the withdrawal period.
- Avoid social events in the beginning if you think you will not make it.
- As soon as you feel better, go out and enjoy yourself.

For those who have gained a lot of weight--eating habits:

Why do so many people eat more when they quit smoking? In my case, I did eat a lot particularly in those three years of off and on because I was trying to fill up a gap or sometimes to make up for a loss. My body was screaming. Fill me. Fill me. I am sure many of you have experienced it the same way I did. You think the longer you eat, the faster the craving will disappear but it does not. On one hand, you have become free from nicotine but on the other hand, this absence of smoking brings you some feelings of emptiness. Though the snack is eaten; it does not make the feeling go away. You still want to fill up a void inside yourself.

So what can you do about that? In the self-suggestion programs, you will notice that I often use the expressions "make the best with what you have" and "one thing at a time". First thing first, each time you eat, eat very slowly and consciously—be in the moment. This means doing just that. Give you this chance. Remember, I told you if you smoke, do just that—be aware of each puff. Well, the same thing will happen with food. If you put all your attention on every bite, you will see that you eat more than you need to. Another interesting thing will happen if you are more aware of you here-now moments. For example, if you do not like what you see after examining yourself carefully in the mirror after a shower or a bath, something will ring in you. Ding-Dong. Ding-Dong. Awareness again. The desire to come back to your normal weight will be greater than your hunger. Again, desire stimulated by awareness will back you up.

However, if you already have a problem with your weight, your doctor will be the best person to help you with this issue. And the more you read about this and look around you, the more awareness you develop. It will be easier to find the right motivation to go on and make your own choices.

If you had told me before that smoking and overeating were illusions, and consequently feelings of insecurity, I would not have agreed with that statement. Now that I know better, I can say that it is. However, I understand that it is very frustrating for people that have an overeating problem to hear that this addiction is another illusion. In my case, it was easier to lose weight because you see I liked more smoking than eating. But for those who like more eating than smoking, the right diet will be important. Here again, your doctor can assist you in your choices of food. Group supports can also make a huge difference in your life.

This SP Freedom-Now method will encourage you to make healthier choices. Never underestimate the power of encouragement because in the long run, anyone performs better when he is motivated to do so. These self-suggestion programs will make you realize that you do not need to smoke at all or eating so much to feel good about yourself and life in general.

However, there is no magic potion for feelings of insecurity. Most of people feel insecure in this world and this, with reason. It is about that we all try to find something to make us feel better.

Lack of nicotine

So now you know that a lack of nicotine often brings an ugly feeling of emptiness at the beginning. And eating more than you need to will not make it disappear. If you eat too much during the day, you will have an awful night. Sometimes, the lack of nicotine may keep you up all night or wake you up in the middle of the night. There are people that get up and eat. In their confusion, they think that if they eat the craving will disappear. And it does. But it is not because they have eaten. **The craving has passed because it is in its nature to pass.** It would have passed anyway with or without putting food in the mouth. That is why non-addicted people call it an illusion. The craving shows up and after a while it goes away.

Illusions

For many smokers, smoking is not an illusion. They will tell you, "You can say whatever you want but smoking helps me stay slim. See I am the proof of it. It is not an illusion." I would reply to you, "Of course, you are right but what a price to pay for being slim."

People who quit smoking usually start losing weight in the same year. But it is also true that some of them keep it on. Doctors, psychologists tell us that smoking and weight are complete separate issues. To me, it is like a catch 22. Some smokers think that when they smoke they are controlling their weight. So they don't want to stop smoking because they are afraid they will be overweight for the rest of their lives. Either ways it looks like they cannot win. Once again the best answer to this issue is reach for help if you need to and use this SP Freedom-Now method.

In those three years of non-sense, I have often relapsed after meeting someone that had stopped smoking and was obese. This would make me run to the store to buy cigarettes. I did not want to be like that. The voice of nicotine would say, "That's right, you see less and less smokers in the street but you see more and more fat people. So make up your mind. If I were you, I would prefer to look grey and thin rather than a big red balloon." You see this nicotine addiction always tries to trick you.

Most experts will tell you that many ex-smokers will gain weight but loose it after a while. Ten to twenty pounds is not such a big deal if you are to lose it in a near future.

Women and gaining weight

For women in particular, this is a big reason to keep smoking. So how can someone stop smoking without gaining too much weight? I would say, "The more prepared you are, the easier it is to do it." Any skilful person would tell you that having the right tools on your side help you do a better job. With this method, you will use your awareness more efficiently. First, you know that you may gain some weight, so accept it as part of the process. Second, your self-suggestion programs will be your big reminder—you will be more aware of what you put in your mouth. And in a short time you will feel so well as a non smoker that you will be ready to face other issues.

As a non smoker, I have learned that I cannot fool myself anymore concerning some types of food. If I have at home things like chips, chocolate, pastries before my eyes, it is hard to resist. So now that I know that for sure, I cannot have these things around—it makes me hungry. If I don't see them, I do not mind. Another thing. Once I start eating junk food, it triggers something in me to have more of the kind. I am aware of it—consequently, I know what to do. It is simple. I go less often to these fast food restaurants. But I am not a preacher, sometimes I do and it is ok with me. Now what I do more often is spending more time and money in grocery stores. Variety in food is the secret. These are my strategies. What are yours?

Benefits of being fit

People in the fitness world often say, "You feel good when you are fit." They are right. Paying attention to the body is important. When you have the right weight, you think faster, you work better and you move quicker. You are more aware and alert. Staying free from nicotine and overeating have no price.

There are other benefits of being fit and keeping active but I do not want to elaborate too much here. I just want to underline that not smoking anymore and maintaining your weight increase your energy and give you a better ability to cope with stress. And of course, you look better by being fit.

At the beginning, it is important to remember that you become tired faster when you lose weight. Here again, remind yourself to take short naps if needed or go to bed earlier in the first weeks, particularly if you feel exhausted. You are renewing yourself. It will pay off soon big time.

You are rich when you have a fit body and a fit mind. Health cannot be bought by money.

CHAPTER FIVE
WHO AM I?

Going through the addiction

The addiction makes the smoker believe that he enjoys it. He smokes because he thinks he wants to. His thinking is full of contradictions. He really believes that cigarettes relax and give him courage and confidence but he also knows it is not healthy. If the smoker forces himself to stop, he feels so tense that he wants to smoke even more. So each time the smoker tries to stop, he finds himself on a roller coaster riding—an emotional roller coaster. To him, life will never be enjoyable again if he really stops for good. It is because he does not realize yet that readjusting to years of abuse will take some time before he finds the right balance.

Going through the symptoms

Once again, the best way to go through the symptoms is to be prepared. You know you will have them anyway—so be ready. Here they are: irritability, hunger, cravings, lack of concentration, sleeplessness, lethargy and hyperactivity, sometimes heart palpitations etc. So the best preparation for the quitting day is getting all the rest you can because you will go through an intense craving for tobacco in the first days.

Being well rested and making up your mind about cravings are your first best two tools. Say to yourself, "I am well prepared. This craving is just a repetitive, insistent thought. My body is just responding to this. It will pass. I can go through it because next week it will be less and less intense." Repeat this to yourself! Encourage yourself! Talk to yourself! During the week, you may go through different states and mood swings. They will not last long, so go through them with full awareness. Feel the pain—you will feel the joy faster right after. The body wants to find its balance. Energy rushes are good signs that your body is freeing itself up from old patterns.

In these first weeks, food will taste better. Enjoy! However, for those who are afraid of gaining too much weight, the self-suggestion programs about personal power and awareness will help you make better choices. But do not forget that withdrawal symptoms will keep you on your toes the first weeks. Give you a chance—you cannot succeed at everything at the same time during the crucial periods. Yes, you will go through nervousness, lack of focus, recurrent thoughts of smoking—but between them you will also experience short periods of calm, well-being and inner joy.

The more aware you become about these symptoms, the better you realize how normal it is to have them. If you stay with the pain when you feel pain and stay with the joy when you feel joy, you are half-way on your path to recovery. After a while, all these ups and downs feelings will make you tired. Give yourself a break. Take a nap.

Breathing too will help you. Whenever you have a craving, try putting all your attention on your breathing, it will facilitate the process of mastering tobacco addiction. Practice, practice, practice.

Now that you are getting better at the business of getting better, each time a thought of having a cigarette pops ups in your mind, pause and enjoy this thought a minute or two. This will make you understand better how a habit works on your mind. Illusion is there—so it means that there is nothing there.

Another thing can occur too in the second or third month. In those testing times, you start feeling better, so you think you are done with this addiction. You go on with your life and suddenly "out of the blue" a mega craving is crashing you. It seems to invade every part of your mind and body. You think, "I just have one." You go to the store and buy a pack of cigarettes. You light one. Right after, you feel dizzy and low. Another relapse.

What to do if you have a relapse? Make a decision. If you still enjoy smoking after all the sacrifices that you have made—go on. Do not feel guilty over that. You will see that the desire to stop will come back and this time, stronger because now you do remember the good moments of not smoking. Keep reading the self-suggestion programs even if you have relapses. Something will click inside of you. I do not know when and how it will work for you but I will tell you how it did for me. I read my self-suggestion programs every morning during the week. Everything was going well until I had a mega craving (the third month). So like a zombie, I went to buy a pack of cigarettes. I lit one and thought that it was not so bad. I was aware of every puff while smoking. However, the minute I finished it, I ran to the washroom and vomited. The month after, I had another strong craving. The same thing happened—sick like a dog. It was the first time in my life that I vomited and laughed right after. I got rid of the pack of cigarettes right away. I knew that tobacco was not giving me anything anymore. Since that last experience, no matter what! Tobacco means nothing to me. It is so great. I am now a happy non-smoker and I have the firm intention to stay a happy non-smoker. To me, getting better at the business of getting better is cool.

How to manage withdrawals symptoms:

As we know the first three to seven days are usually the most intense days of withdrawal symptoms. After that, they became less and less intense. However, periodic cravings will resurface in the first three months. Sometimes, past experiences associated to smoking can trigger the cravings—this strong urge can get you right in the stomach.

It is always a good idea to see your doctor first when you quit smoking. However, you are the only one who will make it happen—quit smoking. Just do not forget that each time you start and stop smoking again, you go through the same symptoms again. But at least now you know how to handle them. Some of you will undergo the following symptoms at different levels of intensity: physical discomfort, mild depression, insomnia, irritability, frustration, anger, anxiety, nervousness, difficulty concentrating, restlessness and impatience.

This SP Freedom-Now Method will be handy here. Each time, you experience difficulties; you will use your self-talk. It will help you manage better angry feelings and behaviour. These self-suggestions programs are great and powerful because they make you aware of what is going on right here and right now. What you say to yourself in the morning usually determines how you day will turn out and consequently, enhance the quality of your life.

However, these self-suggestions programs are not a substitute for anger management therapy. For those who may have a real problem with anger, please see an expert for this issue.

The things you tell yourself in your mind have a very influential part. It is you thinking process that affects how you behave. You may not be aware of its power but when you quit smoking—it is always useful to get a handle on your anger. How? By being aware of it. Before making a scene, isolate yourself. Do not let those you like the most be part of your problem.

Other small issues

When you quit smoking, other small issues may look real and big at the beginning. I think it is important to talk about it. I do remember that in my three years of off and on—not only I ate more but I was constipated each time I stopped smoking. I had never had before any constipation problems in my life. Going through the day feeling bad physically and mentally is very annoying. Fortunately, when I stopped smoking for good, I began to have a better diet. And the body, this wonderful machine adjusts itself one day at a time and everything comes back to normal. Everyone reacts differently—you may not have all these symptoms mentioned earlier. Quitting smoking brings different problems in the beginning to different people.

Grieving

When you stop smoking, particularly the first times, many fears come up about how you will cope with life without smoking. Some people go through a lot of sadness. So the more you know about your fears and feelings, the better you are prepared to go through them. After reading on the subject of quitting smoking and asking ex-smokers how they deal with the symptoms, you will be more equipped when they show their ugly heads. There again, it will be easier if you deal with them this way: one craving at a time—one fear at a time—one feeling at a time—one day at a time. And day after day, you will emotionally respond less and less. If you use these self-suggestions programs one day at a time in the first months, you will become more aware when your body and mind are trying to put you back on your nicotine addiction by giving you reasons to smoke. You will neutralize these cravings by telling yourself that you really have now more reasons not to smoke.

Physical withdrawals

Some people have a very hard time with the discomforts of physical withdrawals. Again, different levels of intensity can be experienced—these symptoms are: tension, tightness, headaches, dizziness, cramps, itchiness, heat, constipation and even nausea. Just remember, they do not last forever. Remind it to yourself often. They disappeared in the first weeks. And GOOD NEWS—no one has ever died from nicotine withdrawals. Ask your doctor.

Before creating this method, I do remember that each time I made the decision to stop smoking—it generated thoughts of anxiety and fear. So each time I stopped, anxiety and physical discomfort would grow and become with the time almost intolerable. When it went on and on, I lit a cigarette and everything came back to normal. Unfortunately, the anxiety stayed with me because it reminded me that I was at square one again and I would have to go through all that torture again if I really wanted to quit for good. So everything became unbearable again—I needed another smoke to deal with that one. It is about that the self-suggestion programs are great. They give you the necessary motivation to stick with your decision.

I deeply believe that I have failed often because I was not enough prepared mentally and physically for it even though I thought I was. When you have all the right tools in your kit box, it is easier to work with this addiction. Even relapses become great lessons—you understand that you will suffer physical discomfort if you stop again but at least you now know that you have a practical method to deal with it.

On your calendar, choose a date. A day you can relax or work less than usual—this way, it will be easier to tolerate the discomfort. You know what it is. You can put a name on this physical threat. You know it will pass. And right after, you will feel better, encouraged, empowered and motivated to go on.

Anger

Some ex-smokers told me that even after a year of not smoking, they still are moody and sometimes they go through a kind of panic. They easily lose their temper. For some, the panic of losing it is so intense and sudden that they are seriously thinking about having a cigarette. I would suggest dealing with it immediately when it happens. Look at it. Have a glass of water. Breathe. Do whatever works for you. And ask yourself why? If you are honest with yourself you will find that you would have dealt with anger in the past by immediately smoking a cigarette. It is important to think about the reason of your anger and what you want to do with it. Let it go or take action. Use the SP Freedom-Now Method. It will remind you that stopping smoking means real freedom and not the other way around.

Depression

Each time you stop smoking, you might experience a mild form of depression. For some it could go deeper than that. In that case, reach for help. Visit your doctor. He will refer you to the right person if needed.

The first month, it is hard to maintain your balance because in your head, you think that smoking a cigarette will lift up your depression. On the surface, you are right. Smoking does help. You feel better.

I went through that many times myself. Each time, I have felt depressed in those relapsing years, I did light a cigarette. I felt better right away even if the taste of nicotine was awful in my mouth and my head dizzy. So what is going on here?

Your doctor would explain to you better than I would what is going on when you go through this physical process. In my case, I usually lit a cigarette when I was tired to feel awful and depressed. You see the nicotine addiction is continually playing with the smoker. Then the smoker tries to convince himself that if he goes see a doctor for anti-depressants, it will not be good for him. It will look bad on his medical history file. What if his insurance or at work decide to check his medical record? No, he cannot let this happen. So he prefers to have a smoke thinking that it will be easier later.

Guilt

Fear, anger, grieving and depression are part of the process for most of the people who try to quit smoking. But here, guilt is a little different from the rest. Some use guilt as a smoking stopper. Is it good? I am not sure of it. Trying to quit can be obsessing. How many of you have said in the past, "I should stop smoking, I am not stupid. I know it is not good for me and for everyone around me. Wherever I go, I look like a monster. Everyone looks at me. It's time for me to do something about it."

And then you get tired of the guilt trip. When the craving is grabbing you, you suddenly shift your thought. You are ready to face the world. You feel alone but you do not care. You do not need others because your cigarette is giving you everything you need. You say silently to yourself when you light your cigarette, "I like it so much. I feel so good when I smoke. I have the impression that I have accomplished something in my life. It really helps me to go on."

Stress

The experts tell us that developing a good stress management is the first step for dealing with any kind of difficulties. How many of you have said in your life, "Smoking helps me relax". The funny thing about nicotine is it is a stress-producing drug by itself. So it is an illusion if you think it reduces stress.

This SP Freedom-Now Method will help you manage your stress level. You will be pleasantly surprised that non-smoking makes you calmer.

When you recognize that you are just reacting to situations and to people, it is time to establish a balance and pay attention to all aspects of life. These self-suggestions programs will remind you to be in the present. You will act more than reacting. Being free of smoke will make you aware of all your needs—mental, physical, emotional, social and financial.

Influence of smokers

Other smokers might affect you once you have stopped. With this method, you will learn how to handle smokers and stay free from nicotine. The self-suggestions about freedom will often remind you that you are free to be and for this reason, you let others totally free. You let them be. It is part of the deal. You accept it for you and so for others. In your own home, you make the rules. However, when you are somewhere else, your freedom is to stay there or leave. You make your choice.

At the beginning, it is true that it is easier if you do not go to places where all smokers are—for instance in a bar where your friends are in the smoking room. But you will handle it more easily with the time and be ok with that. You will understand that these smokers can enjoy their smoking for whatever reason they think they enjoy it and you have nothing to say. What can you really say or do? Stay and enjoy their presence or leave. You cannot correct them but you can say that you are a happy non-smoker. Of course, they will look at you as if you were an alien. Nevertheless, they will take you seriously with the time. You have stopped smoking and they did not—moreover, you did not bitch about that. That will make them wonder about it.

Myths

There are smokers who claimed they do not smoke much anyway. They do not think they are addicted nor have a problem. They will tell you that a few a day do not affect their health. Doctors do not agree with that but this is another issue. However, you do remember you tried it yourself—you smoked a few a day hoping that you could smoke sensibly without it being an addiction and then you ended up smoking like before. You see it is part of the lie of addiction. You hope you can still smoke occasionally. The insanity starts working to make it rational in your brain. The bad habit is preparing its addiction trap. You do remember that each time you felt bad, insecure or fearful, smoking gave you some comfort. You seemed relaxed and free for a short while, and then the bad feeling came back again. You needed another cigarette to cope with that discomfort. Smoking a little is still an addiction. You need it to go on with your life.

Another myth is smoking help you solve problems. Each time, the smoker lights a cigarette, he takes the time to look at things or problems or whatever is bothering him. He seems to deal better with them when he smokes. But he is not. In fact, his little ritual helps him think better, and not the tobacco that he inhales that makes the difference in his way of perceiving the world.

To change your habit with tobacco, you have to change your ritual.

Before stopping for good, I thought that smoking helped me wake up in the morning. I am sure some of you think the same thing. It is pretty foolish when you look closely at it. When you were a child, you did not need a cigarette to wake you up in the morning. You might not be a morning person but if you have a regular schedule—all you need is a new ritual.

After stopping smoking, some of you may feel restless at night. Take heart, the second month, it lessens and then you begin to sleep well. You will see—it will get better and better. After a good night of sleep, you will realize that you really do not need a cigarette in the morning to open your eyes.

For those who think that smoking helps them calm their nerves or provide some confidence are right and wrong at the same time. The inhalation of toxic fumes has certainly an impact on the nervous system. If you want to know more about all the physical effects on the brain and body—ask your doctor. This is not my job. My job is to let you know how I did it and what I understand from my experience.

For thirty-five years, I have really believed that smoking helped me relax and coped with life and anxiety in some ways. What I did not understand was that I created a form of ritual—each time, I felt nervous, I always lit a cigarette. It seemed to calm my nerves. So to me, it was working. Now that I have a new ritual, I know I can relax or cope with life without smoking. You see I did use smoking so many times in periods of stress that I made me believe that I needed a cigarette to go through them.

By the way, stress is there and will always be there. For everyone, there are days easier than others. Each one deals with it the best he can. Reach for help when you need it but I am convinced that inventing a new ritual is a great thing to do. After a while, you will see that it will not be only a new day for you but a new way to look at life.

Once you are a non-smoker
Please do not belittle a smoker because you have made it so far. You know what it is. All right, for some it is easier to succeed than others. Do not fool yourself, you may have let go of this addiction to adopt another one. So respect the one who has a tough time with quitting smoking. You understand the addiction. Do not be a moaner. If you really want to help others, prove to yourself first that you feel better. Live it and everything will follow.

Ways of stopping smoking:
I will talk about it more in detail in the next chapters but for now it is good to know that no matter how many times you quit smoking, you will find that it is different each time. The feeling of the moment—what is going on in your life at that specific moment? Whatever it is, you are going through the same symptoms but in a different mode. So use it for your own good. Pay attention to what works for you.

Sometimes, in moment of mild depression, ex-smokers feel they have nowhere to go, nothing to do, and no purpose in remaining alive. Again, preparing yourself is the best way to go through this without losing it. Having the desire, making the decision and preparing your tool box will do the trick more easily than simply using your willpower. For some, it will be to learn a new way to control the stress with the mind, not with cigarettes. Here are some examples:

- Sit down and try relaxing for a few seconds.
- Breathe deeply.
- Clear your mind, and sit quietly.
- Change your focus of attention frequently.
- Plan more rest and take often short naps.

Stopping smoking is real life. You try, you fail. Try and fail. Try and fail again until you become so fed up of going through the cravings, withdrawals, sleeplessness that you quit for good.

Yet, in the first year, relapses can happen again. Example: you are at a party—you have quit smoking for months. Then during the evening, after a few drinks you decide to accept a cigarette that someone offers you. After a few puffs, you feel dizzy and become so uncomfortable that you have to sit down. You swear it is the last one. The day after, you go buy a pack of cigarettes.

After many relapses, a person in his right mind would ask, "Why does nicotine create so much craving, fear and panic?" If this person is honest, he knows that this craving, fear and panic would have passed after a while and come back again but with less power. What is going on inside is his mind is telling him to light up. If he waits longer than usual, his body will remind him that it is time for a cigarette—so now he feels a mental and physical discomfort. He realizes that his life is one of addiction—a constant nightmare of withdrawal and relief, withdrawal and relief.

Once you understand for good that nicotine addiction is telling the mind what to do and the mind is telling the body what to do and your body is telling whatever it is left of you what to do. Congratulations. This is the sign that you are coming back to life big time.

The right time to quit smoking

The right time to quit smoking is the one you choose. And to repeat again, it is the one you are sure you can have some rest on the first days or at least doing less work than usual. But for the person that has many relapses, the right and good time is always NOW.

I don't really want to stop smoking—you know—social pressure

I know that one. That was my favourite reason for many years. However, evolution did its work, and that reason did not work anymore in my reptilian brain. Another weird thought going on in my mind was I will do everything to stop smoking but I do not want to suffer. We all know that one too. Who wants to suffer? Yes, there are some who do like that but they deal with another addiction. Let them be free to suffer and enjoy!

The social pressure is not a good enough reason to stop smoking. It may make you feel guilty but that is all it does. To those who do not want to suffer, I assure you that if you are well prepared, you will go through that without losing too many feathers and you will fly higher and higher. Once you have tasted freedom for real, there is no coming back.

But before going through this mind shift, it is important to fully realize that nicotine addiction plays on many stages at the same time in the smoker's mind. Sometimes, it feels like this addiction grabs the smoker by the throat when it does not have what it wants—all feelings and emotions trigger a physical response. Some people think that strength and willpower will be needed in that kind of situation. To me, the more you use strength and willpower, the more you will need to fight yourself. I know that many people will disagree with me here but I deeply believe that willpower makes you more miserable than free with the time. I will elaborate about that in another chapter.

To me, the main reason people want to give up smoking is usually because they want to feel better at all levels. So in order to stop smoking for good, you need to do it just for yourself. Others and social pressures are not enough. To help you achieve it, ask yourself often, "What does it mean to me to be a non-smoker?" And write it down. Here is what it means to me.

What does it mean to me to be a non-smoker?
It means TOTAL FREEDOM.
- You do not have to stop what you are doing to have a cigarette.
- You do not have to stand out in the cold on your break to smoke.
- You can sit and watch a movie in a theatre without thinking, "I just feel like going out now and smoke."
- You have control of your life. You can go anywhere you want to and not have to worry about it. It feels good to be free from cigarettes.
- Walking into a restaurant becomes a pleasure.
- You wake up in the morning without a cough.
- When you have a cold or flu, it does not last as long as before.
- It also means you save money or you take time off because you do not have to work so hard to pay for the smoking habit.
- Food tastes better.
- No more constant cough or throat clearing.
- Your fingers are not yellow anymore.

- No need to run to the convenient store late at night to buy tobacco.
- Better sleep.
- No more burns on your clothes.
- You really breathe better.

Of course, you still have bad days but now you understand that smoking will not make your day better. This method can help you solve the problems related to your smoking by reminding you to be in the here and now.

The use of personal power, awareness, focus, freedom and a good sense of humour will help you greatly to do it.

Being a non-smoker means enjoying real life. It will get more and more exciting because you now realize that you have the power to mould it in whatever you want.

Go for it!

CHAPTER SIX
TOOLBOX

How to prepare the toolbox and use the tools:
In order to achieve your goal of freedom, you need to gather all the information and tips about this addiction. From now on, quitting smoking is and will be your goal number one. Other goals can wait. You will work on this one "one day at a time" for about four months before taking off in the real world. This is all you need. Why? Because for the smoker, life revolves around smoking habits. It takes at least three to four months to break it. So if you remove them from your life and feel free and good about it, other issues will be dealt more easily.

At the beginning you may feel like you will never make it—somewhere in your mind, you cannot imagine never smoking again. To help you deal with the discomfort and frustration, you will use the self-suggestion programs first thing in the morning. These self-suggestions remind you that this life is the only one you have. They will tell you to make the best of it with what you have.

If you put quitting smoking for good first on your list to do—I mean your top priority—you are putting the right tools in your toolbox. It is about that I totally agree with AA when they say: First thing first.

I also have to admit that I have stolen this expression from them, "one day at a time". But they did too from somebody else. So I do not feel so bad about it. If I do remember correctly, it came from an old religious text.

After the top priority list and tips, the self-suggestion program is the second most important tool you will use. It will act as one of your big reminder. Every morning during the week, you will start training yourself by reading them aloud. It will implant in you the idea that it is possible to stop smoking one day at a time. But this time, you are the coach and trainee in one session.

"One day at a time" is such a wise expression. It seems easier to take life this way. In fact, if you think about it—it is the only way to live "one day at a time". You cannot go wrong with this one because it always puts you in the here and now. I highly respect AA and the twelve step program. Some people have succeeded to be free from different addictions using this program. However, I also know other people that do not like their program. I will let you judge of that.

If you are still struggling with the quitting day, I mean if you are still trying to choose the right day like before and after the vacation or the holidays and cannot make up your mind, you may stop that by saying to yourself, "There's never a perfect moment to quit—the right moment is now. It won't be easier tomorrow." However, I repeat again: choosing a day where you can rest all day at home works best. If you put yourself in a situation where there is a lot of pressure going on, you will simply sabotage your commitment. And once again, you will be at square one.

When you quit just for today, you will learn to replace cigarettes with different things like a glass of water or juice or a hot beverage—fruits—carrots and celery sticks—or chewing gums. Chewing gum after meals can help you greatly the first weeks.

For those who have a computer and access to internet, you will find out that there are many websites that offer tips on quitting smoking. For those who like AA program, visit their site. They have tips on gaining freedom from nicotine. Read it; it sums up tips you could find on other sites.

Look at quitting as an investment. To me, this is the best investment I have ever made in my life. I can see, smell, taste and touch the investment. This is fantastic.

For those who still have many relapses, take courage. It will click with the self-suggestion programs. When you become so aware of what is going on in your mind, you are more ready to take action in the here and now. The problem with being off and on from nicotine is you are always in a discomfort zone. You are going to hell each time you stop smoking. I know what I am talking about. I had been in this nowhere land long enough to know that it is a just a nightmare. I could not sleep. I could not relax completely. I gained and lost weight fast which made my skin sagging and flabby. I felt limp. I had no energy. I lost my zest for life. I did not feel like going to work. I had a hard time to focus and concentrate. When you write, it is pretty discouraging. I spent lots of money on different things like books, tapes, nicotine patches, nicotine gums and so on. And then tired, I would buy cigarette cartons and put them on the credit card. I did not want to know how much I was spending on cigarettes anymore. At the end of the road, I was not just broke in the pocket but in the heart.

Now, I understand completely that this nicotine addiction was pulling the strings. My thirty-five smoking years were stronger to break than I thought. But how could I know any better if I had nothing to compare with in my past. I could not remember the way it was when I was a child. But fortunately, I have learned of that nonsense of off and on. After trying so many different things, methods that did not work at all, one day, fed up, I decided to make the best with what I had. That day, I created a method that worked for me.

These persistent relapses have shaped and framed for me a new way of thinking about this nicotine addiction and at the same time about decision, choice and illusion. Here is an example of that process: when you make the decision of quitting, you are glad that you finally made it a commitment but you also think that letting go of nicotine will deprive you. In your mind, these two thoughts come and go. If you want to reverse this defeatist monologue, you have to use all you have—it means your awareness and personal power. Awareness and personal power will let you know that you are making the right choice. Choice to feel better instead of depriving yourself.

When you stop smoking, you feel a void—so it is important that you drink lots of water at the beginning. Why? Because it fills up physically your momentary sense of loss. Being aware of it, each time you drink liquid, informs your brain that you are doing something about that.

And yes! Do not think you will be a nice person the first day you quit smoking. Even if you are the nicest person on the block, you will go through this phase like everybody else which means feeling cranky, crabby, or plainly angry and physically uncomfortable. If you can manage to be alone on the first day—good! At least, you will be the only witness to your misery. And of course, the first week, you will feel easily annoyed by little things. However, if you are fully aware of it, you can minimize the damage by telling others around you and by paying attention to your little whims.

The first week you do not know what to do with your hands. In this case, take a pen and keep it between your fingers like you will for a cigarette. I have found that it helped me a lot when I was reading something. However, after a while you will not need to do it anymore.

Another tip that can help you is avoiding becoming too tired. You become impatient with others and yourself and regret things that otherwise you would not have said or done. Sometimes, for no reason, you will find yourself bursting out crying. It is about that I say that you need all the rest you can in those first weeks. For instance: if you are at home, when you start crying of nervousness, sadness and rage, go lie down and cry all your heart out. Each time a craving points its ugly head, take a short nap, lie the time it would take for you to smoke a cigarette. Then get up and move.

If you feel very anxious, angry, resentful, and short naps do not work anymore—put some rock' and roll music on and turn up the volume. Dance until you cannot move anymore (any fast tempo music will do). I prefer rock' and roll music because to me it is the only music where you can let go and have a good fight with the invisible smoke.

Walking is very good too. Make sure you always have a bottle of water with you and sip it. And as I mentioned earlier, chewing gum or sucking candies can tremendously help you at the beginning. Now the good people will say—chewing gum or sucking candies are not good for you. Let them be. They have scared you enough in your life.

Take breaks often. Sometimes, all you need is a distraction to shift your focus from a craving.

Avoid negative people, and places that make you uncomfortable especially in the first weeks.

Go to places where you are sure you cannot smoke like seeing a movie, visiting a museum, going shopping etc.

When you are at home and you feel tense, relax in a warm bath or take a long shower.

If possible, hang around non-smokers a lot the first weeks. Do something with them like swimming, hiking, going out with them.

Each time you feel like putting something in your mouth, choose to bite into an apple or carrot, celery—cinnamon sticks, sugarless gums, candies or lollipops. Choose anything that works for you.

Give yourself rewards frequently. It takes a lot of guts to change and break the nicotine addiction.

Remind yourself often that your personal power and awareness will support you in your choices. As soon as you quit smoking you will notice you are breathing more freely. You have a good breath. Your clothes do not smell anymore the old tobacco. If you are on a bus or in the elevator, you will know right away if someone smokes. It is something you did not pay too much attention before because you thought you did not smell too much. You now realize that other non-smokers can smell it easily.

I have read that some smokers' cough may increase temporarily during the clearing process but will subside with the time. That was not my case. But if it happens to you, you now know that it is normal.

Here are some more tips you may add to your toolbox:

Tips:

- Change your routine often.
- Motivate yourself with the self-suggestion programs. They will support your efforts as a non-smoker one day at a time.
- Get rid of things that no longer serve you.

- Change everything you possibly can the first month. After it, balance yourself with your likes and dislikes.
- If you want to be a happy non-smoker, you will have to schedule a time for bitching, swearing, screaming and being simply a jerk. **No witness is necessary.**
- Learning to relax is one of the best tools you can use against stress. Do not fool yourself—it takes time and a lot of practice to make you believe that you deserve it.
- When you feel overwhelmed, your body might tighten up. Take a big breath and realize where you are. This means here and now. The more you are aware of being in the moment, the easier you are able to cope with pressure and demands as they arise.
- Walking in the open air will benefit your health and energize you.
- Laughing is another wonderful tool to make you realize how good life is without smoking. Having fun will be part of your daily life. Enjoying yourself as a non-smoker will be your first priority.

You had a ritual when you smoked. You will now create a new one that fits you like a glove. This new ritual is another important tool in your toolbox.

Here is an example of ritual:
1. At the minute you wake up, drink two full glasses of water—thirsty or not.
2. If you are used to have a bath or a shower in the morning, do it.
3. Drink whatever you are used to drink in the morning—coffee, tea, orange juice, etc.

4. Sit down. Take a few deep breaths before starting the self-suggestion program. This one lasts between fifteen to twenty minutes (see the next chapter to know how to use the programs). These self-suggestions programs are designed to help you not to lose it completely the first months and feel better about you. You can repeat your program as long as you want but no more than thirty minutes. The reason is simply not to get bored with it. Just do not overdo it.
5. Have a good breakfast. Eat slowly.
6. As soon as you finish eating, get up and go brush your teeth or chew a sugarless gum. Anything that can help you to ease that after meal moment.
7. Get ready for the day.
8. Be sure that you always have a small bottle of water with you everywhere you go. Take often little sips. Thirsty or not.
9. If you face a lot of pressure in the first weeks, make sure you have on you sugarless gums or candies—anything that can help you to go through the day.
10. In case of lack of concentration—try to be in the moment even if you have to bring you back to reality many many times.
11. If you are at work, as soon as it is possible, take little breaks. Ex: go to the washroom, etc.
12. Eat and bite into fruit and vegetable—apples, carrots, celery, etc.
13. When you are living great moments of stress, force yourself to concentrate on one thing at a time. Say it to yourself, "One thing at a time".

14. When you feel the pain of nicotine withdrawal, stay with the pain. Be aware of this kind of pain only. (I noticed that the following days were less painful when I was doing it.)
15. At home, take often little breaks. Lie down only ten minutes at a time if you like (the time of a cigarette). Get up and try to distract yourself.
16. Have a walk outside if you work at home, etc. If you do not like exercising, dance on dynamic music. Improvise. Find methods to let out your aggressiveness, anguish and anxiety.
17. At the end of the day, reward yourself. You deserve it!

Important: If you are a nicotine patch or gum user, or in relapse, you can still start this SP Freedom-Now Method. It will help you make a final decision and motivate you in your desire to stop smoking for good. You will be pleasantly surprised of the effects that these self-suggestions will have on you.

However, I cannot repeat enough that stopping cold turkey is very difficult the first days but twice easier after it.

When it comes to quitting smoking,

Willpower is not enough. Most of the ex-smokers that have stopped smoking with their willpower still think about smoking, dream about smoking, and envy others when they smoke—and that after many years. If not, they have probably replaced it with another addiction. Addictions play with your willpower. To me, willpower may work for a while but people who only rely on their willpower are often unhappy fellows. It is true they have stopped smoking but at what price. They are miserable, and they will stay that way if they do not change their ways of seeing things. How do I know it? I know it because I tried it. I also witnessed other people using it. And moreover, I have done my own little survey and asked ex-smokers. Some of them told me that it is still there somewhere on their mind—I mean fantasizing about smoking. As I mentioned earlier, I like to call them the willpow-pow people.

This SP Freedom-Now Method uses personal power instead of willpower—big difference. And in addition, this method is for people who want to be happy non-smokers and stay happy non-smokers. So the best way to know if you are a happy non-smoker is by asking yourself if other smokers bother you when they smoke close to you. Now you know where I want to go. It means that you realize after a while that your desire for smoking is gone and it will not come back even in the presence of smokers. My method wants to demonstrate that desire and decision of quitting smoking help you take the necessary actions with fewer side effects—and the self-suggestions back you up in your actions.

When I started writing these self-suggestions, all I wanted was to find words that would support me in my desire to be free from nicotine. After testing these statements, I was pleasantly surprised to see right in the first month that they reminded and motivated me to stay free during the day. So I kept writing for three more weeks on the same topics—personal power, awareness, focus and concentration, freedom and joy. I became so aware of what I was thinking and doing that lighting a cigarette to deal with whatever I was facing did not make any sense anymore. That was it. I said to myself, "Wow! This method really works."

A word about cold turkey

At the beginning, it is true that it is difficult to use the cold turkey way but if you stick with it and have your own little ritual and do the self-suggestions each morning—it will be so easy after that. And do not forget that you are well prepared this time. You have your toolbox with you and the right tools in it. However, if you find it hard to do it alone, please feel free to get all the help you can. Reach out. Talk to your doctor, a counsellor or a therapist etc. Some people will prefer to have a support group. Again, these are tools you can add to your toolbox. I am sure you have heard before that when you have the right tools, everything is easier to work with and you do a better job. We can apply the same principle with quitting smoking.

About all these nicotine replacements, it is true that people use them in order to reduce the intensity of symptoms but as soon as they stop using them, the intensity of cravings comes back. So again, it just prolongs the torture. Sometimes, speaking to the right person like an ex-smoker will do more good than the replacements. This person understands what you are going through and can find the right words to motivate you enough to stay free when you feel bad.

Reminders

Just being aware of the habit of smoking is a big step toward kicking the addiction. Again, if you are still smoking, do not do other things when you smoke, just smoke. Do it with every cigarette. Sit down and smoke. Each time you stub out, say, "Bye-bye" to it. Then go back to whatever you were doing.

The goal is to encourage you to enjoy yourself more in all you do.

You will find that each time you have a relapse and start again being smoke-free, symptoms will be slightly different. Sometimes, the withdrawals will be more or less intense. Everything has to do with the mental and physical shape you are in. Ex: you may find that this time is easier to stop smoking while other times, you are suffering weeks of depression.

It is often fear that keeps us smoking. Smokers fear that life will never be enjoyable again without tobacco. They already feel deprived even before trying to stop smoking. Fortunately, millions of people and I can assure you that it is quite the contrary. Life is not only more enjoyable—it is like day and night. All your senses are more alive than before. You feel more energetic, strong and powerful. And you have lots of fun too. You do not need anymore this little tobacco stick to stimulate your wit.

Remind yourself before having a smoke that smoking is more than a bad habit, it is a drug addiction. It is drug because you have to have a smoke to operate in life. If not, you feel like a total failure. Do you remember those days when you were sick having the flu or a cold at home, and you were still reaching for a cigarette coughing like crazy? This is an addiction. Now, I call it insanity. You feel sorry for yourself but you are still smoking anyway.

Smokers think that smoking relieves boredom and stress and gives them more concentration and relaxation. If you still find yourself in a kind of void after months of non-smoking, it means that you are not convinced that you have made the right decision. For some, one of the reasons they start smoking again is they feel healthy but miserable. They ask themselves, "What is the point of being healthier and richer if I am so unhappy?" Their misery is not related anymore to withdrawals or cravings. They feel like it because their mind is still telling them, "You don't enjoy life anymore because you stop smoking. Everything is now dull and depressing." They become stressed just thinking about it. And now, they are down. But there is a better way to deal with this kind of melancholy. Your awareness. Checking your thoughts in the here and now will do it. In these down moments, have the courage to ask yourself, "Are these thoughts helping me or letting me down?" Your awareness will sift them out for you.

Relapses

Most of people who have quit smoking for good have tried many times before succeeding. The good thing about your relapses is you have learned a lot from you and them in the ring. And now, just like a boxer, you are better prepared for the next round. You know what to expect. You know that drinking plenty of water will help you flush faster the nicotine from the body and satisfy oral urges. You have learned that holding your breath for twenty seconds or more eases discomfort from nicotine withdrawals. Just doing these simple things makes the urge pass more rapidly.

We all look for an easy way to stop smoking. However, when you are not aware of what works or does not work, you waste time relapsing and staying in that awful state of sickness. Once you find what is right for you, you understand how easy it is to stop this nonsense of torturing yourself. Life gets better and you are more motivated to leave behind this smoky illusion for good.

If you have tried using only your willpower to stop smoking and it did not work, it is because you force yourself to make sacrifices. Some succeed but they are often the grumpy ones to avoid in a party.

When you do your self-suggestions programs, you start feeling stronger and stronger. Awareness finally pays off and the real fun begins. You do not abuse your new freedom like you did in the past when having relapses. You take the time to be in charge. You know when it is time to stop and relax—when it is time to work—when it is time to sit down and reflect.

Create your ritual

There are periods when smokers can handle long periods without smoking. Why is that? They seem to do it effortlessly. The reason is simple. They know they will smoke right after that. It will be their reward. So they can wait because in their mind, they link life with work, pleasure and rewards.

Now the question is, "How can you be satisfied and rewarded without smoking?" My answer to this is by creating a ritual that includes finding satisfaction in the moment and rewarding yourself with a real thing.

For those who are still smoking, I know that a lot of ex-smokers like me have succeeded by cutting down cigarettes in a relatively short period, by being aware of each puff while smoking, and by creating their own ritual.

As I said earlier, you have a ritual when you smoke. Think about it, it is almost religious and sacred each time you light a cigarette. Now all you have to do is to create another ritual for your new you and your new life. Make it sacred if you like. Nobody will interfere with your ritual.

To refresh your memory, go see, "Here is an example of ritual" page 71.

If you do not like this one or it is because it does not fit with your schedule, write one that will work just for you and stick with it in the beginning.

Reading aloud your self-suggestions programs will also help you be more in the here and now. Your concentration will stay more focused on what you are doing. And you will feel more encouraged to stay free from nicotine one day at a time. To me, these self-suggestions are a very good starter in the morning and seem to ease the day.

Another important thing to remember: reward yourself on bad or good days.

Relaxation and pleasure

The belief that smoking helps you relax is the biggest illusion of all. Because if it is true that smoking helps you wake up in the morning, then there is a problem here. A big contradiction. The smoker in denial will say, "Oh! Yes. Smoking does different things for me. In fact, smoking helps me wake up, concentrate, lose weight during the day and stimulate my brain. And yes, it also helps me think faster, work better, socialize, be more satisfied with my life and relaxed."

And with a big smile, this smoker will add, "Do you think that I am ready to give up this wonder drug that gives me so much. Go to hell with your illusion. I know it is not."

I know it is a weird and funny thinking but we all had been there before. So!

Another thing. Please do not force those that are in denial "to see the light". At the beginning, in my enthusiasm to having found something that worked, I would let people close to me know that my method was working well. However, I have learned something important from that: when people are in denial, everything becomes an excuse when it comes to quitting. Some of them said to me, "It may work for you but I don't think it will for me. Anyway, I'll try on my own. Thanks but no thanks." I understood. They are still smoking but I let them be. If they do not want to help themselves, that is all I can do. Let them be.

Other things that can help you stop smoking are relaxation techniques. There are many different methods on the market. Books, DVDs, CDs, Yoga teachers, etc.

Good news about quitting

It feels good to be a quitter when it is for a good cause. After only four months free from nicotine, you will find that it is easier to rest and relax—and the fact that you do not depend on the drug will empower and calm you down. Imagine no more guilt or shame over harming yourself. This is great.

Another good thing to underline is once you are free from this addiction, you do not desire or miss a cigarette after a meal, and you celebrate the total eating experience. You really appreciate what you eat. And then, you smile. You cannot believe that you have lied to yourself for so many years.

When people that had never smoked in their lives were telling me how bad smoking was, I used to say, "Smoking is my only pleasure in life. Please, leave me alone with it." That was not entirely true but that was my ready-to-say answer to them. I also remember having had depressed periods in life when I was flat broke—however, I had always managed to have cigarettes. I hated rolling but I would roll them if I had too. I always made sure that I had tobacco first with me. Tobacco would go before food, paying bills, drinks and things needed. It was usually for a short period of time because filling my nicotine addiction was my priority, and I was better to move quickly to make money.

After a day of hard work, I would sit and smoke a cigarette. I would say to myself, "It tastes so good. I deserve it and it's my only pleasure in the moment. I cannot afford anything else, and food makes me fat anyway."

Now you see that it is important to reward yourself often. You have to give yourself the pleasure of tasting life at its best. Everyone has his own pleasure, own way to satisfy oneself. After a hard day or a good day, whatever it is, reward yourself the best way you know. Sometimes, little things you buy in a store will do more than a big meal in a restaurant.

And once you are completely free from nicotine, you understand how and why this addiction has deeply affected your life for so many years. You realize too that relief from withdrawal is one big pleasure you give yourself not the opposite.

Again, different things will be treats for different people. Every day, reward yourself for a job well done, for another day free from nicotine. It can be anything, a small thing like doing nothing in the morning, reading a good book, seeing a good movie, having a good meal etc. Remember, everyday is a cause for celebration.

On your monthly anniversary, congratulate yourself for all the hard work and good effort. Find a way to give yourself a real treat and celebrate your success.

Continue to work with your feelings and enjoy your new health. Remind often yourself that you are moving forward and let go of the past.

Use your success as a non-smoker to realize other goals. You now know that if you are able to be a non-smoker, you are able to accomplish many other things. And you know that it was not your willpower that did it but your desire to do so. Your desire brought you the determination necessary to do it, and your motivation made it possible.

Celebrate your freedom every day. Sing it, dance it, and laugh it. Enjoy! Quitting smoking is a good marker from the old you to the new you.

Even if you have tried to quit and failed many times before, you have better chance of succeeding through the use of this method with fewer side effects.

The last words on toolbox
- Mental preparation before quitting is important. Planning in advance how you want to quit can make a big difference.
- Pick your day. Look for a day when it will be easier for you to relax and have support. If you cannot make up your mind—choose today. Now is the best day to quit.
- Sometimes, the support you get helps you a lot. Find people to talk to. Go online. AA meetings for nicotine addicted or other kind of support groups. Often, other ex-smokers are the only ones that understand the tumultuous storm going on inside of you. These ex-smokers will encourage you to hang on, will tell you that these feelings will disappear in a short time and they will not come back.
- Create your ritual step by step. Write it down and stick it on a place where you can see it. Make sure you have not forgotten anything. If you make it a big project, you will have more chance of success.
- Think about what situations make you want to smoke, and plan how you will cope with each one.
- Learn what to expect and how you can make it better. Irritability and nervousness are common withdrawal symptoms. Deep breathing and water help many people cope with this.
- When you make a conscious decision about quitting and courageously follow through it, you feel so good. Even if you fail after a while, it is a success because you are ready to try again. This is "real spirit". Never give up.

- When you quit smoking for good, something extraordinary happens: you feel like you now can do many things that in the past were challenging you. You learn practical ideas to solve problems.
- If you have succeeded to make that change with nicotine, you can make changes in other areas of your life as well.

Once again, quitting smoking means different things to different people: for some, it may mean to summon the inner strength to take action in spite of fear which in return may help you confront the hard problems of life. For others, it may mean to set realistic goals and create action plans—or simply enjoy the feeling of inner peace because they now live in accord with their values and belief. Peace and freedom have no price.

We learn a lot about life when quitting smoking. Personally, what I have learned from quitting smoking is making the best of any situations with what I have. I do not succeed all the time but I become more aware of what is going on in and out myself.

Each time I remember to make the best of it, I feel better and smarter.

Living in the present moment is the only way for making it "the best of it".

What to do if nothing is working for you

When you smoke, do it alone. Smoke your cigarette consciously. Concentrate on every puff. Focus on the smell and taste. Feel the smoke going down through your lungs and coming out. Each time you put it out, say, "Bye-bye" to it. And now concentrate on being free from slavery. Unlock the chain mentally. In the morning, go read the self-suggestion program. Even if you are still smoking, read your self-suggestions programs every morning during the week. Something will click. Pretend that is your best coach or new you talking to you. Believe me you are a new person after stopping smoking. Moreover, when you are healthy and cheerful, smokers respect that and they envy you with the time.

There are now so many public places that smokers are not allowed to smoke that some of them begin to panic. There is a change in society. Smoking is now regarded as an unsociable habit, even by smokers themselves.

You know you cannot go back in time anymore. Why torturing yourself with that?

CHAPTER SEVEN
THE METHOD

What it is:

This method is the most important tool in your toolbox. In this box, you already know that being well prepared is part of the first compartment. In the second, you have a new ritual to follow on the first day. Then with all the tips and ritual on your side, you go to the third compartment, There, you find your self-suggestions programs. On your quitting day, you start reading aloud or whispering to yourself in the morning a series of short statements. It lasts between fifteen and twenty minutes. These programs will accompany you the first months. What are these statements? You may ask. I will tell you right away they were made for a specific goal: freedom from nicotine. So do not worry, they are not farfetched. They are down to earth. They always put you in the "here and now" and make you aware to live "one day at a time". With these programs, you put all the chances on your side. And what happened to me can happen to you. After doing these programs on a regular basis the first month, I became free like a bird. No more crutches.

Now, I know you are a little disappointed and you say, "I will have to read them in the morning during the week. Why don't you make a CD of them and this will be it?"

My answer is, "No, I won't." Why? Because CDs and tapes don't work. It may seem to work the first times you listen to them. It gives you a kind of enthusiasm and puts you in a good mood for an hour or so but when you try to quit smoking for real you just want to throw the CD through the window right after the first week. Well, I know. Tried it—done that.

If you want this method to work for you, you have to do your homework by reading the self-suggestions to yourself during the week. You have to hear yourself telling it to you. Of course, you can write them but you have to write them for the day you are about to live if you want it to work. This is the way my method works. It is simple. When you do the work, it works!

I said many times in other chapters that the easier way to quit smoking is the "cold turkey" method. It is hard the first days but it gets easier right after it. It offers less suffering and creates a shorter period of withdrawals. When you use patches or gums, you still have nicotine in your body. This means it is easier to relapse—and you still have withdrawals even after a month on these replacements strategies.

So when it happens, you are back to square one. And if you replace smoking by any other addictive substance or food, you are fooling yourself.

Nicotine is a powerful addictive drug. Smokers must recognize that they are **drug addicts**. "One day at a time" is the only way to quit. This concept is taught by almost all programs which are working to deal with substance abuse or emotional conflict of any kind. The reason is it is simply easier to handle. So "one day at a time" makes sense. And it works almost for any traumatic situations.

Of course, never take another puff one day at a time will work but if you are a rebel like me, you will need more than that. In order to stay free from nicotine, you need more than a nice slogan, you need to summon your personal power to make a decision and stick with it. Again personal power is not willpower. It is more than will power. In these programs, my definition of personal power is the ability to do and act on a goal by using your head, heart and talents. So with your personal power, you use your awareness to know what is going on inside and outside of you. You use your focus and concentration to go through the day without losing it. You use your heart to go for it with all the guts you have. After a short while, you are fully aware that personal power brings you the motivation necessary to go on with your goal.

If you have a relapse, never, ever feel guilty about that—disappointed maybe but not guilty. Why? Because there is no moral to this story of relapsing. And by the way, moral has killed more people on this planet that nicotine did.

But one thing I can tell you for sure is there is life after smoking. Of course, you will have bad moments every now and then. All kinds of situations can occur—like experiencing stress at home or at work, or being in a pleasant social atmosphere that will trigger an unexpected craving.

And ding-dong, the desire for a cigarette will knock at the mind door. How will you answer? Well, I hope you will kick it where I think you will or stay with the feeling of the craving. You know it will pass anyway. So move. Move works.

This method intends to show you how to let go of this addiction—the bad smelly habit that is holding you back and robbing you of your freedom.

As you read I know that you are resisting. I do not have to be a psychic to know it. I am an ex-smoker, and nicotine has no more secrets for me. Resistance is one of the biggest obstacles on your way to freedom. Once you learn to let go of resistance, your life will begin to flow with greater ease and clarity. As a non-smoker, you will feel happier for no reason. I repeat for no reason. You might even find yourself waking up in the morning like a child, happy to start the day. Not bad if you were a rebel!

Some therapists say that when you know exactly how the addiction works you are on your way to freedom. To me, it makes sense but it does not mean that you will go for it. After reading books on stopping smoking, I have learned a great deal of how this nicotine addiction works on the body. How the brain responds to withdrawals, etc. However, it did not help me stop smoking. I think I smoked more after that. And each time, I saw ads using fear on TV showing the bad effects of tobacco and hammering them over and over—it just made me smoke more after it. First, rebellion took over and then gave place to discouragement and guilt—of what—of not being able to quit on my own.

You see what I really needed to know was what is going on at the mental and emotional level. I needed support. I did not want to hear—smoking is bad, it will kill you—I already knew it. What I needed was motivation, encouragement from my mentors—not telling me how many people died from it—how smoking causes all kinds of illness—how I will suffer all my life if I do not quit smoking right now—how stupid I am to keep smoking after having all the information in my face. Ok, you got it. Me too. Smokers are rebels. They don't like having an authority—so rigid in its way of thinking—to tell them what to do with their lives.

What I really wanted to hear was—how wonderful quitting smoking was, how marvellous and joyful it was to the mind and body. It sounds too over the top for you—just teasing you! However, it is true that quitting smoking puts you in control of yourself and your environment—that breathing better makes you feel better and gives you the motivation to create and do things. And it is also true that day after day, you are getting better and better—you feel freer and freer—and you look better and better. No, this is not New Age—it is No Age! There is no age to have fun.

I am glad to have found a good way of breaking free from this addiction. This method made me realize how many false beliefs I maintained in my mind about tobacco. For example, each time I was facing a difficult time in my life, I was so used to automatically light up a cigarette thinking it was helping me go through it. Now I know there is a better way to deal with it without lighting up. You see for the smoker's ritual, lighting up a cigarette seems to start the whole process of thinking. In the first week of quitting, YOU THINK YOU CANNOT THINK WITHOUT A CIGARETTE. And you are right because you have an addicted brain. In your mind, it is difficult to think without some **smoke in the brain.** It is weird! **You think you need some grey fumes to make you think clearly.**

These self-suggestions programs will help you to be aware of your thinking process. And you will learn, the more you practice thinking about a situation without having a cigarette between your two fingers, the faster you will know what to do about it. It can be doing nothing or doing something. Your awareness will give you an answer. In your addicted mind, you think that smoking does many things for you. Once you quit smoking for good, you are forced to realize that smoking never made you more intelligent, brighter, smarter or wiser. You are or you are not. Period.

The smoker thinks that smoking gives him the stimulation necessary to take action on a daily basis.

When you stop for good, you will be surprised to find yourself taking the right action faster because you feel better. The rebel that you are will still be rebel—but now you know why. There are so many causes on this earth. Pick one if you like. If not, stay a rebel without a cause. Everything is up to you!

So now you know that your big helper will be your self-talk. I have made these self-suggestions to support you the first four months. The best way to use them is first thing in the morning during the week from Monday to Friday. On weekends, you are free like a bird. But if you find them helpful, do something different. Choose the statements you like and copy them, or write your own. Something that fits you—something that is more personal and sounds truer to you.

Cds do not work when it is about stopping smoking. I have tried them and I asked other people—they do not work. Do not take my word for it, try it. Your personal effort in the "here and now" works a lot better. So reading aloud or writing down your statements is the best way to do it. However, I would like you to stay with the five topics I have chosen. There is a reason to it. You will understand what I mean right after doing the self-suggestions the first week. The way I have designed them is to make an impression on your mind that will stay in the background all day. When you read aloud these statements, do it in a low voice almost whispering—like a child learning his lesson in the morning. Each week you will have a different set of self-suggestions and that, for four weeks. So you will never get bored. When the four weeks are done, you return to the first programs and start doing them again. On Mondays, the self-suggestion program talks about personal power. On Tuesdays, the program is about awareness. On Wednesdays, it is about focus and concentration. On Thursdays, it is about freedom. And on Fridays, it is about joy.

Personal Power

What does personal power mean to you?

Answer this question the best you can. It will be your code of surviving for the rest of your life.

To me, personal power is using all I have—my desire, my guts and my willingness to do it. This is not willpower like courage is not willpower. Smokers that are using the willpower method are putting themselves in a very difficult situation. They are trying to forget about smoking. They think that after going through days without smoking, they will eventually forget about it but nicotine addiction does not work this way. After a few weeks, the willpower starts failing and the depression sets in. The willpow-pow people cannot sleep anymore. They lose their temper. They become anxious and then give in. Willpower means to me self-control—sacrifice—winning at all costs—winning even if you lose your mind. Being right is more important than being happy. Now you know that I really hate this word "willpower" with a passion. Personal power is rather a combination of desire, wisdom, determination and motivation. You use your head and your heart. Willpower wants you to forget while personal power goes with you through your umpteen cravings. You feel the pain, you stay with it. You even savour your cravings. You remind yourself of the joy of not having to choke yourself anymore.

When you wake up in the morning, you get clear with the fact that in life there are good and bad days whether you smoke or not. Personal power will deal with it better than willpower will. If you do not believe me—you are free to use your willpow-pow.

So to recapitulate: after making the decision to stop smoking, you use the personal power technique to prepare yourself mentally to go for it. You gather all the tools and start working with them. When you do it the way you want and it works, you feel good about it.

And when you feel like having a tantrum, please reach for your toolbox instead of using other people as targets of your anger. Do something. Go isolate yourself for a while and breathe. Go for a walk or run. Put energetic music on and dance your heart out. Punch a pillow or cry your rage. Any technique to get it out of the system will do.

With this method, even if you have relapses, you feel good. It means that your start appreciating that you feel good with or without smoking. After experiencing both situations, your personal power and awareness will make the difference. You will see, after a while, you will feel better when you do not smoke. It is about that it is important that you do your self-suggestions even if you have a relapse. Something will click as I said earlier. It will follow a pattern. You will begin to analyze your feelings while you are smoking them. Your right mind will start seeing the real thing. Then, you will realize that non-smoking means only benefits.

This is the beauty of it. You cannot lie to yourself anymore. You quit. Then, one day, you light up again a smoke. The taste in your mouth is awful, you feel dizzy, and you have nausea. You had that before but this time, it is different because it really tastes awful and you are really sick. No matter what, you do not feel good anymore about smoking, and somewhere in your mind, you are glad that it happens because you know right at that moment you can do easily without. You start to feel good again. Your personal power is waking you up. Your focus and concentration backed up by your awareness is letting you know that you have earned your freedom. You get rid of that tobacco immediately and easily. And then, weeks after weeks, you feel better and better. Joy is rescuing you. Rejoice! This is not New Age—it is No Age. There is no age to feel good and have fun.

Awareness

Wakefulness, knowingness, consciousness, condition of being, etc. For the purpose of this book, I define it by being aware of what is going on inside and outside of you. Awareness is what you sense about yourself, others and life. If you want to know more about it—read books about awareness or go online. Here, awareness is used as a tool. It will remind you to be in the Now. The first week, awareness will seem to be often on and off. However, with the time you will begin enjoying it—you will simply be more alert. Your awareness will "put you together" so to speak. The self-suggestions on awareness will motivate you to be in the present moment. It will stick in the back of your mind for the day. Of course, from time to time, you will still be oblivious of it but you will come back faster to yourself. Two other tools that will help you stay in that state are focus and concentration.

Focus and Concentration

Focusing in the moment will help you do one thing at a time. So when you concentrate your attention on what you are thinking, it will be easier to focus on thoughts you enjoy and drop the ones you do not.

For example: each time you have a thought of anxiety, rage, hatred, craving, worry, judgment, resentment—any kind of thoughts that bother you—first, you do not judge them, you just look at them for what they are, no more, no less. So one thought at a time, you use your awareness to decide what you want to do with it. Keep it or let it go. You will see—it clears out a lot of space on your mind. By the way, this same awareness will also focus on the little joys you feel in the moment.

Keep reading the self-suggestion programs in the first months—they will help you make the right decision and stick with it. Some of you will continue smoking but I am almost sure that one morning you will be so fed up, so tired of the ceaseless struggle, you will realize you do not enjoy smoking anymore—you just do it by habit.

With these self-suggestions, you will start being so aware of your body and what you are doing that the idea of smoking a cigarette will not come up as often as before. Here, it is almost a done deal. Moreover, practice makes perfect. When you practice enjoying everything you do during the day—smoking or not—you enjoy it—it will be easier to explore the pleasure of doing it in the here and now.

A good way to practice is pretending that you are a non-smoker for an hour, a day or whatever. Start considering what it feels like, you will see that you can come up with different strategies each time. When you act like a non-smoker, your inner freedom takes its place. Look at it as a new adventure.

There is a lot of information out there for smokers who want to stop. Health agencies and other associations like Canadian Cancer Society, Canadian Lung Association, public schools, and others are giving out lots of information in order to educate smokers and let them know how terrible tobacco is. **Why then, smokers do not quit if they are so well educated about the terrible effects that nicotine has on the body? It is because smokers are still enjoying a lot their smoking.** To me, if you want to be a happy non-smoker for good, you have to enjoy more not to smoke. Quitting without joy feels like something is missing in your life. But when you are a satisfied and relaxed non-smoker, you feel whole again. You fully realize that nicotine made you believe that you could not survive without it—you now know that it was just a lie. To feel good and free is a wonderful feeling. Happiness is a very serious business. This is not New Age. It is No Age. Ageless Wisdom.

In your toolbox, preparedness is the first tool. You are mentally ready to quit. On the quitting day, you know for sure that your thoughts will start racing—however, you will not panic because you know that you have a good plan to back you up. Consciously or unconsciously, the first week, you will search for good reasons to start again. You will even tell yourself that you are about to give up this non-smoking non-sense. Whatever you think or do, talk to yourself—say that it will pass, encourage yourself, and reward yourself. And one hour at a time, you will make it happen. Your body circulation, your breathing and digestion will begin to improve immediately. Day after day, you will feel better.

A last word on concentration. In the past when I smoked, I really believed that smoking helped me concentrate better. I also thought that smoking gave me inspiration when writing or creating things. Then, I went through these three years of on and off—it was very difficult to write or read but as soon as I quit smoking for good, I built up my strength. Now that I am free from nicotine, I know that it was a big illusion. My focus and concentration are better than before.

Freedom

Give you the freedom to change. Each time you smoke, and think how stupid it is, freedom is not far away. You still like it but you do not know why anymore. Your nicotine addiction is filled with contradictions. You have put up with it for so long that you do not see them anymore. The key to your freedom is seeing between your contradictions. They will fight each other as long as you desire. If you can stay with your cravings, fears and pain long enough, it will pay off. Cravings will come back but with less intensity. Sometimes out of the blue, a big one will show up—if you accept it as part of your way to freedom, it will go away as fast as it came.

It takes courage to become free from any kind of addiction. But once you have decided with your head and heart to stop smoking, the desire will lift you up. From that moment on, it will be between you and you and no one else. You will do it just for you. You will be so mentally and physically prepared, you will just jump in. Your desire and self-suggestions programs will be there to back you up with your decision.

And day after day, you will feel better and better, you will feel freer and freer, and you will look better and better. Can you ask more than that?

Joy

Joy can be described as a very glad feeling, delight, happiness, pleasure, etc. I told you before that with this method, being a happy non-smoker and stay a happy non-smoker is not farfetched. If you use your toolbox properly, you will be very satisfied with the result. Being happy here simply means that you do not miss anything anymore from smoking. To me, this is real joy.

The self-suggestion programs on joy make you appreciate that you are free from nicotine one day at a time. They also make you realize how addicted you were and how good you feel now. So you can live more deeply the little joys of the day.

The Best of yourself—what it is?

The Best of yourself is you at your best. It is not too complicated. Being the best of yourself also means being your best friend. Here in these self-suggestions programs, you are your own coach, your best friend.

Another way to illustrate the Best of yourself is by going back in the past. I am sure you remembered days when you felt at your best for no reason. Everything worked well together. You were aware, alert and focused. You just felt like singing and dancing in the street when going to work. You enjoyed others and yourself completely. You got the picture!

It is possible to live those moments again. How? By using your best friend to work for you when your little self cannot. When you cannot take it anymore, you will give it to the Best of yourself—it will not be a burden anymore for you. Here, believing or not will not interfere with your beliefs and values. However, if you give whatever is bothering you to the Best of yourself and are aware that you are doing it—you will feel that there is something going on there. Just watch, you may feel lighter by the simple fact of letting go. You will not just think that you are letting go—you will be aware of it. It means that you stop every other thought and put all your focus and attention on that thought for a few seconds and then forget about it. This principle seems to work very well when you are aware of doing it. I know it will be tough to be aware of it the first days when you have a lack of focus and concentration. Take heart. A way to facilitate it is to remind you often to be in the moment no matter what.

One day at a time, you will recognize more easily when something does not serve you in the moment. Getting rid of it will be your letting go. These self-suggestions will help you live in the here and now. The past is the past, the future is the future. All you are is really in the moment. However, do not be discouraged if you think that you are not there yet, because I am not in the present all the time. Great spiritual masters will tell you that it is almost impossible to be all the time in the moment. I mean to be completely aware of it. On the other hand, you will be more aware when you are not in the moment. So it is a plus. You will enjoy more and more what is going on around you.

Emotional feelings like sadness, fear, anger, guilt, resentment will come and go more intensely during the first week. It will be a little tough and almost impossible to deal with them all the time. However, you know what to do—the more you remind yourself to be in the moment, the better you get at it. Then later on, you will be more focused and relaxed. You will use your awareness technique: one feeling, one emotion at a time. Little by little, you will gain emotional freedom and you will feel physically better. These same feelings or thoughts will come back on their own in your lifetime but then you will not need nicotine or eat more to deal with them. It is also very important that you know your limits like when you get too tired, you know that you are fragile or vulnerable to smoke again. Have as many short naps as you like. Plenty of rest. Do not feel guilty if you think you have not accomplished too much on that day. It will pay off later at all levels.

There is a change in the air. Can you smell it?

These self-suggestions will help you retrain yourself. They will give you a new way to look at life, practical and down to earth. When you quit smoking, you start a brand new life. It is a new adventure through smell, taste and even touch. You feel more alive.

So between two cigarettes, start playing your role as a non-smoker. Pretend. Each time you have a craving, say to yourself, "What's wrong? I don't smoke." Keep doing that as if this craving was trivial—even if your whole body is shaking. If you cannot take it, go lie down.

In these first months, you will deal with lots of weird thoughts—good or bad. Do not be offended. You were addicted to a powerful drug! Each time you have a lack of concentration; remind yourself that nicotine may act as a stimulant but at the same time it plays with your behaviour and bang! You get hooked again in the process. Nicotine addiction makes you think you really need it to deal with the ups and downs of life. The problem with that is you always need it to feel good. Smoke has made you a slave. The SP Freedom-Now Method will help you program your mind and body to feel better. And better thoughts will replace the old tape. After a while of doing your self-suggestions, you will start enjoying more your new freedom. A feeling of well-being will encourage you to appreciate life more right here and right now. You will feel lighter and joyful simply because you are more truthful to yourself. You will have more satisfaction one day at a time.

One more thing—I want you to know that I do not agree with quitting methods that try to scare you to death. In fact, I cannot care less about people who are at wars with tobacco. Lots of smokers, the rebel ones smoke just to despise the warriors. When you quit smoking for good, you do it for yourself not for others.

But one thing is sure, you cannot fool yourself anymore. After years of puffing, you realize that you have put yourself in jail. Everything turns around your smoking habits. It is a never-ending life of slavery.

I hope that this book has clarified the illusion of smoke for you. If so, you will be like a magician. The nicotine-make-believe will not work anymore because now you know all the tricks. You are well prepared and you have all the tools to perform. I am sure that you will do it with style and grace.

The statements on personal power, awareness, focus and concentration, freedom and joy will generate a deep conviction in you, and things will begin to happen. You will become more consistent in your effort. You will experience a greater sense of joy and satisfaction in your personal and professional life. Your quality of life will get better and better and you will be doing more the things you like. This is pretty cool!

CHAPTER EIGHT
THE SELF-SUGGESTION PROGRAMS

How to practice your self-talk script

The best way to practice it is to pretend that it is your new you that is saying these self-suggestions to you. In these four months, you will be your best friend, or the best coach you will ever have.

It is very important to know that if you just read these statements once, nothing will happen—absolutely nothing. It is all in the way you do it.

You will read aloud each program almost whispering it to you—as if you were a child learning a lesson or if you like an actor reading a script.

The best time to do them is in the morning. However, if you have a different schedule, choose a moment that fits you best during the day. Find a place where you will not be disturbed, have a drink and sit down. Take a few deep breaths. Each program lasts between fifteen (15) to twenty (20) minutes.

Each program includes a set of fifteen (15) statements written in the "first person".

The first time, you read each statement three (3) times in a row.

The second time, you read the fifteen (15) statements just once and you start again.

The third time, you replace "I" by "you". "You" here serves as validation as if it was your best friend or coach talking to you. So you read the fifteen (15) statements once and do it again with "you".

The fourth time, you come back to "I" and read the fifteen statements. Then you repeat once again.

You are done. You will see—it will stay in your memory all day and will facilitate your task. And all that, in no more than twenty minutes. You can take thirty minutes if you like to but no more than that. The reason is simple: if you overdo it, you will get tired easily and give up.

After four months, you will not need these programs anymore. But maybe like me once in a while, you will do them just for the fun of it. They seem to put you in a good mood and prepare you for the day while reminding you that you are now free from nicotine. Sometimes in life, we forget we have accomplished great things. Quitting smoking is one of them. In fact, it is a giant step. Each day, celebrating the freedom from nicotine is a nice way to remember it.

These self-suggestions will reinforce your decision and support you through the day. And as I mentioned in other chapters before, if you still smoke—read them aloud anyway. It will help you more than harming you. The only thing I will ask you—smoke before or after—but not while you are reading it.

When you do your self-suggestions programs every morning during the week, you will feel like you are taking charge of yourself. This in turn makes you feel better. And each time you feel good, you have personal power—you are getting better at the business of life.

When I say four months of using these programs is enough, what I really mean is it is up to you. For some, it will take three—for others, six months. Everyone is different. However, we all have the chemical and emotional dependences in those first months, so it is important that you do them on a regular basis.

So each day of the week—Monday to Friday—you will read aloud a new self-script. For four weeks, you will have a new set of self-suggestions every morning. Even if they are on the same topics, they are different. It will be more interesting this way. When you finish reading it the first month, you start again the same process the second month and you do them until you feel that it is enough. You are the only judge of it.

Do not tape it, it will not work well. What works is when you hear your voice live one day at a time: when your ears hear it from you here and now. You see the words and you read them aloud. You can write them down if you like to but just for the day. You need to make this effort if you want to help yourself. Each morning, you will hear your fresh voice telling you what you want to hear anyway. To me, they are not affirmations but self-suggestions because they are telling you why you are doing that. Your brain will pick them up more easily because they are making sense and they are simple, practical, and down to earth.

These self-suggestions refer often to the Best of yourself. Here, I would like to clarify something about it. It is not the higher power that AA groups refer to. Nothing wrong with this. But I had something else in mind when I say the Best of yourself. You are the best of yourself by simply doing the best you can with what you have. I introduced you to that concept before. Just remember the good moments in your past where you were on top of the game without trying too hard. Days where you were alert, focused, efficient and joyful or times you felt directly connected to your environment. In those days, you were at your best and now it is time to have more of that. When you stop smoking, you will see that it feels good to feel good. No more smoke filters to interfere between your mind and body.

Now you understand that these self-suggestions programs are coping techniques. You now have them in your toolbox. They will be handy when you deal with emotional loss, frequent cravings, relapses, time distortions, etc.

And I would also like to add that these self-suggestions written in this book seem very simple, almost too simple at first look. Do not worry, they are weighed and thought according to their efficacy. By writing and practicing these self-suggestions, I have understood that the more simple and natural they are written the easier and faster the brain receives them.

You need all the help you can get when you stop smoking. **A visit to your doctor first** is always a good idea. If you cannot go "cold turkey", your doctor will help you make the right choice. They are many nicotine replacements available on the market like patch, gum, inhaler, anti-depressant Zyban, etc.

You know what I think about them but I must admit that I know people who have succeeded with these replacements. So...Others prefer alternative therapies such as hypnosis, acupuncture and herbs. If it works for you, good! If nothing works for you, this SP Freedom-Now Method can change your life. Give it a good try. You will see.

I think that people come back to smoking (even if they really wanted to quit) because they did not have enough good moments. If you feel miserable most of the time as a non-smoker, life becomes unbearable for you and others, and you give up. This technique of self-suggestions works because it makes you realize that you have the power of choosing and doing it in a pleasurable way.

At the end of the first week of reading these self-suggestions, you will lightly notice that you are alert more often. It is true that it will be difficult the first two weeks to maintain your focus and concentration while reading, listening or doing things but the third week, the mind and body will be more balanced and then it will get easier. During weekends, do something different. If it is just rest—rest. Or enjoy the company of your friends, read a good book, cook a good meal—anything that makes you happy and distract you from tobacco. And reward yourself often. Buy yourself lots of little gifts and pamper yourself.

If you relapse, try again and again. You now know what to expect and you are more prepared. **Use your toolbox** and deep breathing, awareness, water, gum, self-suggestions, dancing and laughing a lot. Stretch out your meals, eat slowly. Change your normal routine, take time to walk, pamper yourself. Have a long bath, listen to good music. Think about being here and **do it here now.** After meals, get up and brush your teeth, use a mouthwash to have another taste in your mouth, or chew gum, or go have a walk. To deal with mood swings, learn to relax. Lie down and do nothing. Remember, the urge to smoke lasts only a few seconds, it will pass.

These self-suggestions will often remind you to celebrate life one day at a time, free from nicotine. They will also signal to the brain that you know what you are doing and it is better to listen because this time you mean real business.

Life is life. Sometimes, the ride is smooth. Other times, it is simply awful. All of us are faced with grief, loss and struggles. Instead of reaching for a cigarette to deal with it, reach for the Best of yourself. It will remind you that you are the one who calls the shot. Give everything you do not want to the Best of yourself, it knows what to do with it. I know it sounds weird but it works. It is like there is something in us that knows what to do with what we have and use it to the max. I call it wisdom. The best of yourself is the wisdom in you.

CHAPTER NINE

SP FREEDOM-NOW METHOD SELF-SUGGESTIONS PROGRAMS

First week

Program 1.1: Personal Power – Monday

1. My personal power is always in the here and now.
2. I know what I want and where I am going.
3. I have a clear, sharp and organized mind.
4. I am aware of my personal power.
5. I have the ability to do what I want with energy and strength because I am physically fit and my mind is there to back me up in all my steps.
6. Living in the present moment reinforces my personal power.
7. Everything I do is the result of my decisions.
8. I am alert and aware. My mind is clear. I am in touch with everything around me.
9. My source of power comes from the Best of myself.
10. It is my strength, my force and my source of energy.

11. I feel good about all my decisions. My life has more meaning to me now.
12. All the small actions I take everyday change my life for the better.
13. Every time I want to make a change in my life, I write it down, set a goal, review it daily, act on it, and achieve it.
14. My goals give me a clear picture of my future.
15. I am financially independent and free.

Program 1.2: Awareness – Tuesday

1. I am aware of my inner dialogue. I listen to myself carefully.
2. I begin to pay attention to what I think. If I don't like it, I change it for something more in harmony with who I am.
3. I live my life by choice, not chance. Being aware helps me make the right choices.
4. One day at a time, I work with what I have and make the best of it.
5. I change my negative self-talk with awareness. I replace it with what I really want in life.
6. I use my awareness to correct bad habits, focus my attention and live in the here and now.
7. I understand that thoughts are just thoughts. Therefore, I have a choice in what I think.
8. I know that awareness and practice are the only way to change my thinking about nicotine.
9. I am learning to be more aware of what is going on in my mind.

10. I am also aware of the little joys I am feeling during the day.
11. My awareness about my mind and body gives me a higher level of consciousness.
12. My body is intense, wondrous, pleasurable and powerful. I realize that I don't need to smoke anymore in order to be happy.
13. I practice enjoying everything in my life. I practice being here now.
14. I am more satisfied with my daily experiences because I explore the pleasure of being here now.
15. I am here now, and I enjoy every minute of it.

Program 1.3: Focus and concentration – Wednesday

1. What I focus on expands in my life.
2. When I stay focused, I reach my highest level of potential.
3. One day at a time, I focus on what I am doing—I improve my confidence and performance.
4. When I am facing a big challenge, I breakdown any large tasks into a series of small tasks and start taking action.
5. I am in complete control of the concentration of my mind. I unite all my senses and bring all of my awareness into focus.
6. Every day, I prioritize my activities, and I focus on one task at a time.
7. My focus is like a "mental tune-up". It clears my mind and improves my memory. It develops my thinking and concentration skills.

8. I practice directing my attention, focusing my thoughts, and maintaining full control over my mind.
9. Concentrating is consciously focusing my attention. When I give something my attention, I am able to give it my complete attention.
10. I have an excellent memory because I listen completely and clearly.
11. When I find myself too often distracted, I focus all my attention on my breathing.
12. Wherever I go, I am ready. I experience life as it unfolds, moment by moment.
13. I think clearly because I concentrate only on one subject at a time.
14. Each day, I develop my problem-solving and brainstorming skills.
15. At night, I am able to relax. I am at peace with myself and with life. I consciously remove all unnecessary thoughts from my mind and let them quietly go.

Program 1.4: Freedom – Thursday

1. I am breathing the fresh air of freedom.
2. I am so glad I am a non-smoker. I feel free, energetic and healthy.
3. Today and every day, I celebrate my freedom from nicotine.
4. I am ready for new ideas and new things to do. Amazing possibilities are presented to me.
5. I am a work in progress. I have the firm intention to be a happy non-smoker and stay a happy non-smoker. Time to change things in my life and explore new ways.

6. Each morning, I feel good and free. I realize too that I now have more strength and courage to face the day.
7. During the day I feel revitalized and rejuvenated. Being a non-smoker feels great.
8. I don't overwork—instead, I determine my priorities. I know what actions to take moment by moment.
9. I can go now anywhere I want to. It feels good to be free from cigarettes.
10. To love myself is to live at my best. Inner freedom is real freedom.
11. One day at a time, I stay smoke-free. I now have money for the real things I need in my life.
12. I am more in control. I sleep better. I really enjoy being here and now.
13. I see my freedom as a gift. I use my freedom responsibly.
14. Freedom is the oxygen of the soul. I am breathing the fresh air of the eternal now.
15. Freedom from nicotine has changed my life. Today, I am a new person.

Program 1.5: Joy – Friday

1. Joy is my only truth. Here and now is my only reality.
2. I enjoy life and life enjoys me. I make joyful connections—I have fun with what I am doing now.
3. One day at a time, I celebrate every step of creation. I find solutions and make it work.
4. Sharing my joy with others is the best thing I can do for myself. People respond in the

same way, and it creates an uplifting atmosphere.
5. I am a happy and healthy non-smoker. I like the new me that is coming through.
6. Being a non smoker has only benefits—I enjoy the effects on me here now. Every day I feel better and better.
7. I am now fit and healthy, and I like what I see when I look at myself in the mirror. I feel successful.
8. My joy of being depends on nothing else outside itself. I am who I am. I feel within me the good that has no opposite.
9. Enjoying myself is the most important thing for me and for everyone around me.
10. I now find joy in the moment. I enjoy more excitement, success and personal satisfaction on a daily basis.
11. I learn that the best way to stay joyful is to help others achieve their dreams.
12. Being joyful brings light into my life, and it is something I naturally share with others. Laughter is after all the best medicine.
13. I sing and dance to that. I take life as it comes and make the best of it.
14. One day at a time, I experience the joy of feeling good.
15. I am open to more joy, enthusiasm, imagination, playfulness and creativity in my life.

Second week

Program 2.1: Personal Power – Monday

1. I trust myself. I have faith in the Best of myself. Life is now becoming truly exciting.

2. I am learning the joy of taking control of my own life.
3. People are important to me. I am understanding and considerate of others.
4. I always treat others the way I want to be treated.
5. I am able to express my feelings in a healthy and positive way. I am in control of my thoughts and emotions.
6. I begin each day with a clear mind. I organize my thoughts, and I take full responsibility for every decision I make.
7. I now concentrate on those things that are important to me. I am proud of myself for taking the time to take control.
8. Every day I activate my personal power by taking action on those things that I want.
9. Each time I take action, I bring myself to a higher level of energy and awareness.
10. I never forget that personal power without wisdom is nothing. I make sure that I follow a path with heart.
11. Life is my only real counsellor. I am wise and listen to it.
12. I empower myself when I trust my feelings and my guts.
13. I stop dreaming life and I live it.
14. My joy now becomes the focus of my life.
15. One day at a time, I enjoy life to its fullness, and I feel good about it.

Program 2.2: Awareness – Tuesday

1. Every day and in everything, I feel creative, clear and inspired.

2. Here and now, I achieve deeper awareness of my being.
3. I think faster and perform better when I am totally in the present.
4. I only focus on the task for better results.
5. One day at a time, I reap the benefits of my awareness: I feel more satisfied with my life. I reduce stress, and I am more emotionally stable.
6. Whenever I am facing a difficult situation, I breathe deeply. I think it through before acting.
7. I often remind myself during the day to take deep breaths. It helps me enjoy the moment more intensely.
8. Each day, I also take a little "playtime" to refresh myself.
9. I like to find new and exciting ways to be my best.
10. The future is now. The best way to predict the future is to create it now.
11. One day at a time, I plan my work and work my plan.
12. I am fully present at this very moment. Life is a journey, and each moment is precious to me.
13. I am aware that what I say to myself is important. If I don't like it I change it for something I really want.
14. Each moment, I make the best of whatever I focus upon. I repeat that often to myself: make the best of it—make the best of it.
15. I fully celebrate my freedom from nicotine. I feel stronger and more alive. Life is good!

Program 2.3: Focus and concentration – Wednesday

1. I train my mind to be deeply relaxed and sharply focused.
2. I am now able to concentrate for long periods of time. I take control of my mind.
3. The skill of relaxing and concentrating my mind at any time and for any reason is my gift to myself.
4. I improve my concentration significantly by practising on a regular basis.
5. Becoming a non-smoker is one of the most important decisions I have made in my entire lifetime. I was aware of my choice—I focused on it, and acted on it. And now, one day at a time, I celebrate my freedom.
6. In any decisions I make, my self-suggestions give me a strong support when I need to take action.
7. I believe in my ability to do whatever I like to do.
8. Each day, I renew my mental energy by doing things I like to do. It enables me to focus and concentrate better. I am more creative and I improve my imagination.
9. My mental abilities focus on my intuition and reasoning for solving problems. The better I understand a problem, the clearer I am able to see its solution.
10. I know what to do and when to do it, I am organized and in control of my thoughts, my time, my actions and my present.
11. The more I focus in the moment, the easier it is to cope with pressure and demands as they arise.

12. I am not afraid to walk new paths. I have made the decision to become the very best of who I am. This is how I choose to live my life.
13. My goals are clear now and I know where I am going.
14. When I wake up in the morning, I know that I am starting a new day and new life. It is great!
15. I have more energy and stamina than ever before. I enjoy life and I am feeling good.

Program 2.4: Freedom – Thursday

1. My true freedom comes from the Best of myself. I breathe it every day.
2. The more I experience my freedom from nicotine, the better my quality of life is.
3. I have opened the door to my freedom, and I don't look back anymore.
4. Today, my life has more meaning to me. All I want is to enjoy life the best I can.
5. I am now free to use my abilities to improve all areas of my life.
6. One day at a time, I start life with a clean slate.
7. My awareness, my focus and my personal power help me stay free.
8. I began realizing what is really important to me. I now create these moments that I will treasure for the rest of my life.
9. I often remind myself that personal power and freedom without wisdom are nothing. I say only what I mean, and do my best in the moment. I let others be, and I enjoy being free.

10. Real freedom is led by wisdom. Freedom and wisdom are known to me just in the now.
11. I take the time to think through any decision I make. When I deal with a problem, I keep my mind alert and open to all solutions.
12. I free my breath, I free my life. When I breathe deeply, I relieve stress and increase vitality. It helps me live more fully.
13. I find freedom within myself. It is a state of mind and heart, not dependent on any circumstances.
14. One day at a time, I feel the lightness of being through me.
15. I want to live my life to the fullest. I know that what I get out of it is what I put into it.

Program 2.5: Joy – Friday

1. Connecting to people and having fun are things I can make happen today. I am up to it. I look forward to it, and I am doing it.
2. I know where I am going and why I am headed there. I choose to walk on the road of freedom and joy.
3. One day at a time, I adjust my life to what I am facing. Courage backs me up, and I know I am not alone. I ask for help when I need it.
4. I cheer up to my freedom from nicotine. I am breathing the freshness of the eternal now. I give thanks for all my blessings. Life is good!
5. I now realize that all the little joys of the day are the source of my happiness.
6. I am ready to grow and become more joyful in all areas of my life.

7. Today, I give myself a mental makeover by activating my inner joy. It is in me and on me wherever I go.
8. I am creating the "me" that I see in my mind by doing the best I can today.
9. One day at a time, I let go of things that don't work for me anymore and welcome the ones that do.
10. I express myself freely. I make a commitment to being authentic. When I embrace the truth in my life, I start experiencing more joy and success.
11. I now create space for more joy in my life. I let go of the past. I look forward. I support others who want to get real with their lives.
12. I align myself with who I am now. I am a happy non-smoker. I improve my physical and emotional health. I reduce stress by not living up to the expectations of others.
13. Joy gives me more energy to do things I love. I create time for leisure and pleasure.
14. I am in harmony with my true, natural and authentic self.
15. One day at a time, I believe I can create win-win situations in my life. Joy is the source of this mutual benefit.

Third week

Program 3.1: Personal Power – Monday

1. I experience a sense of power when I feel in control of my life.
2. My power is in the ability to think by myself.
3. The freer I am, the more powerful I become.

4. My personal power is in the capacity to pay attention to the here and now. I generate my energy by only doing this.
5. My personal power is in the power of making choices.
6. I choose to be healthy, fit, loving and wealthy.
7. I choose to be true to myself, and achieve my full potential.
8. Being myself means becoming the best I can.
9. It is time for new ways of thinking and new ways of doing things in my life.
10. My personal power unlocks the door to lasting changes and puts me in control of my own life.
11. I make the first move and the Best of myself does the rest.
12. I am discovering what really matters to me now.
13. I have a renewed energy and confidence. I am learning to act—not just react.
14. I am learning to find solutions to any situations I am facing.
15. I deserve the best, and I have the firm intention to get it.

Program 3.2: Awareness – Tuesday

1. I am in complete control of my mind, body and health.
2. Every day and in every way, I am getting better, wiser and more beautiful.
3. When I wake up in the morning, I feel free and more enthusiastic about my day.
4. I love and appreciate myself just as I am.
5. I accept all my feelings as part of myself.

6. I do my best and understand that we are all doing the best we can.
7. One day at a time, I can handle changes that come my way.
8. I respect my personal needs and take time for balance, recovery and good nutrition.
9. I think and act in ways that make me feel more positive and confident.
10. To be here and now means that I improvise each minute—I remain open to the creativity of the moment.
11. I am aware that the best of myself backs up my every move. It is my best connection with the universe.
12. I pay attention to my thoughts. I don't judge. I let go of those thoughts I don't enjoy. One thought at a time—one day at a time.
13. All my physical senses come alive when I begin enjoying more of my thoughts and feelings.
14. Every day my health is improving, and I feel more joyful.
15. I feel good about myself, about life and about others. I am ready!

Program 3.3: Focus and concentration – Wednesday

1. One day at a time, I improve my focus and direction. I achieve more and I am becoming more confident.
2. Focusing helps me balance different areas of life and have a better quality of life.
3. My health is improving one day at a time.
4. I approach new situations with a clear mind. I am effective and efficient.

5. I pay attention to what people are saying and what is going on around me. It pays off because I now have an excellent memory.
6. My personal power, my awareness and my focus back up my decisions. I am free to grow, to change, to take risks, to rise up, and to create a better life for myself.
7. I focus on solutions rather than problems. I am more optimistic and have more energy than before.
8. I really like breathing clean fresh air, being healthy, and being in complete control of my body and mind.
9. I enjoy being a healthy non-smoker at all times and in all circumstances. My sight, my sense of smell, my hearing and my sense of taste are more alive than before.
10. I not only focus on my work but on things that make me feel good.
11. I reward myself for my successes.
12. All things are now working together for good in my life.
13. When I focus on the job at hand, I perform better. This brings me deep satisfaction.
14. Every day I improve my focus by doing things that highly interest me.
15. I am the director of my destiny. I know where I am going and why I am going there.

Program 3.4: Freedom – Thursday

1. The more I know myself, the freer I am.
2. I am free when I think by myself and make my own choices. I control my own mind.
3. The best way to love myself is to take care of myself.

4. I am free and respect others in their freedom. I let them be.
5. One day at a time, I achieve my personal freedom. I know what to do when I feel trapped: first, I stop and listen to what is going on in my mind. I start being fully aware of my thoughts. Then, without judgment, I give them to the Best of myself that knows what to do with them. I let them go.
6. I now understand that I am free to succeed the way I want, and I am also free to fail. It is the only way to know if it works or not.
7. Every day, I exercise my freedom by being aware of my personal power.
8. My life is my own. I accept the responsibility for my success.
9. My choice is my own, and I know what I want. The path I follow is always my own.
10. I experience freedom when I enjoy it. I give thanks for living in a free country, a free society and a free world. I am a free spirit.
11. I am capable of moving and turning in any direction. I feel confident on the road of freedom.
12. One day at a time, I am focusing on getting well. My freedom from nicotine helps me do just that.
13. I get my personal needs met first, so I am freer to be fully with other people and ideas.
14. I am willing and ready to take action to change those areas in my life that are not working for me.
15. I live in the now. Today, I will find a way to make today count.

Program 3.5: Joy – Friday

1. One day at a time, I am walking on a healthier and more joyful road.
2. I am ready to face and change my reality. I now reach for help when I need it, and I help when I can.
3. Each day, I connect better with others. I improve my relationships. I stop blaming others, and I listen to them without judging.
4. I sense a profound change in myself—I now have a new perspective on life. I am creating a new way of thinking.
5. I am deeply grateful to all the people who have helped me on the road of freedom.
6. True joy is pure wisdom. It is the key to a joyful and productive life. I often remind myself of it.
7. I understand too that others are doing the best they can with what they have. I am free, and I let them be.
8. I am learning something new every day. It helps me stay curious about life and others. It stimulates my mind to create new ideas.
9. Creating is fun. Happiness is an inside job. When I feel lost, I reclaim my power by understanding that I place too many demands and expectations on myself. So I keep it simple.
10. When I feel stressed, I cope with life by doing one thing at a time and getting the rest I need when I need it.
11. I have made the decision to grow through joy. I don't take myself too seriously. I say bye-bye to drama. I hang out with people

who have a good sense of humour. Every day, life is getting better.
12. Today, I am in a good mood, and I have the firm intention to stay this way. I will deal with problems one at a time. Nobody will interfere with my decision to be the way I want to be today.
13. My personal power and my awareness set me free. I am here to celebrate life, and I will do it properly. Nobody will stop me.
14. In the morning I ask myself—how can I bring more joy into my life today? Ideas are flowing through me as I start enjoying the moment.
15. I never expect perfection of myself. I only expect the Best of who I am, and I enjoy being me.

Fourth week

Program 4.1: Personal Power – Monday

1. I know that I have personal power when I feel good. In these moments, I know that I am successful at the business of life.
2. I accept myself right here and right now. I am patient and understanding with myself—this is my gift to me.
3. I am practical and realistic, and my feet are on solid ground. Today is a great day, and I have got what it takes.
4. I like to find creative ways to do things.
5. I use all my talents and capabilities to accomplish my desires. My mind, body and spirit are now working together as one.
6. I make decisions for myself, and I am responsible for my own actions.

7. I choose to work for what I believe in.
8. I am totally independent of the good or bad opinions of others.
9. I am calm, and my mind is at peace.
10. I know what to do and when to do it, and I do everything I need to do when I need to do it.
11. I enjoy getting my life in order because now I am in touch with who I really am.
12. I practice listening, understanding and being supportive. I care about people and other people care about me.
13. I think, act, feel and live differently now.
14. All my senses are clear and alive. I feel good and relaxed. I enjoy being a non-smoker at all times and in all circumstances.
15. Today is the day that I find joy in my life. So I live today, today.

Program 4.2: Awareness – Tuesday

1. Every day, I consciously enjoy more and more my life. I can feel that my senses are becoming cleaner, clearer and more acute.
2. I am aware that enjoying myself is the most important thing for me and for everybody around me.
3. I am glad I am a non-smoker. I now see the new me that is coming through.
4. I often remind myself to breathe deeply when I feel suddenly anxious or have an immediate craving. It helps relieve the muscular tension.
5. I am becoming more conscious of my habits patterns and what my feelings and emotions are. Thereby, it enhances my effectiveness in the world.

6. Each day, I become more aware. My awareness helps me let go of negative emotions more easily.
7. My self-suggestions are reminders and reinforce my intention to stay free from nicotine.
8. I am my own best friend. I stop living in the past and start enjoying my life right here, right now.
9. My life is filled with love, joy and health. Love is a state of being.
10. I say YES to what is and take my attention deeply in the now.
11. When I wake up in the morning, I say to myself that I am ready to live this day with whatever I have. I use each minute gracefully.
12. No matter what it is that requires the very best of me, I can do it, and I know I can.
13. I look forward and don't look back anymore. I have the ability to focus on one thing at a time. I concentrate my attention on my task.
14. Today and every day, I reward myself for being a non-smoker.
15. I can do whatever I want because I don't hold back anymore.

Program 4.3: Focus and concentration – Wednesday

1. I am mentally prepared to live and perform my best, consistently.
2. When I am faced with setbacks or distractions, I come back to myself quickly and regain control of the situation.
3. A focused mind is a powerful mind. One day at a time, I am learning the power of

concentration. I eliminate distractions and sharpen my focus.
4. When I use my very sharp "laser-like focus", I feel more energetic and extremely alert. Whatever I do, I do it with confidence and inner joy.
5. I am free from nicotine—I am now fit and healthy, so I perform better.
6. Every day, I think more clearly, I become more creative, I learn faster, and I have a stronger memory.
7. I am now able to find inner peace.
8. I concentrate more easily because I am interested in what I am doing.
9. I also realize how easy it is to concentrate when I do one thing at a time.
10. When I focus on one thing at a time, I immerse myself fully in the present moment rather than the future or the past.
11. My mind is clear, and I move forward with new confidence. I seize the opportunity.
12. I like to create new and better ways to solve problems and deal with life situations.
13. My awareness helps me keep my mind open to all solutions—and solutions come quickly to me.
14. One of the things I do to eliminate worry from my life is to take action today on those things that require my attention today.
15. I value myself, and I believe that I deserve the best of myself.

Program 4.4: Freedom – Thursday

1. I am a new person today. I look at the world with a fresh and open mind.

2. I enjoy my freedom of expression and action here and now. Freedom is the natural right of all human beings.
3. Every day, I open my mind to new ideas, new challenges and new solutions.
4. I find ways to feel good about my life. When I am frustrated with a task, I remind myself to make the best of it. I ask myself how I can make this funnier, easier, better and faster. My attitude changes when I do that.
5. Each day, my new life brings me a fresh start.
6. I see all the benefits of my freedom from nicotine. I feel better, I smell good, and my life is improving at all levels.
7. I am proud of myself and enjoy my smoke-free life.
8. Every day, I practice my new freedom. I am interested and curious about others. I want to know more about what is going on on this earth.
9. I am learning to use whatever I have to make my life better. I use the power of now to make things happen.
10. When I feel discouraged, I take a break. I rest or do nothing special. I just let myself be. I take care of myself. There is a time for everything in my life.
11. I always feel stronger when I choose what I will do with my freedom.
12. The way I like to experience my freedom is to be all here at this minute. It is so refreshing and liberating.
13. Every day, the Best of myself shows me what I am capable to do with my life. I surprise myself all the time.

14. I always make sure that my road keeps going. I know who I am, what I am doing, and where I am going.
15. At night, I sleep well. I like to imagine myself floating on a cloud free of worries, free of anxiety. I wake up in the morning fully rested.

Program 4.5: Joy – Friday

1. I believe in myself. I am never afraid to try. Today, my awareness and joy back me up in everything I do.
2. Being a non-smoker always adds to the joy of the moment.
3. When I feel sorry for myself, I stop and say, "Rather than focusing on what is wrong in my life, I focus on what is going well for me.
4. I forgive myself for anything I have done in the past that I don't feel good about. The more I do that, the easier it is to open the path to joy.
5. I feel free today. I own my life. I am the one in charge. Nobody will take my joy away from me.
6. I appreciate all that I have. I focus on what is working in my life. I have so much to be grateful for.
7. I can laugh at myself. I accept myself totally. I like to laugh and play. I smile at life and life smiles at me.
8. One day at a time, I experience peace, joy and serenity. I feel good about myself and others.

9. I often reward myself for being a non-smoker. I am proud of me.
10. Joy is an attitude—it comes from a feeling of inner peace, and the ability to give and receive.
11. I can now handle with grace the situations I have considered difficult in the past. I am starting to blend with the Best of myself now.
12. Joy comes when I decide to grow through joy. Today, I choose to be with people who respect me and have a good sense of humour.
13. I am glad to be alive. Today, I will remind myself that life is too short to waste and too precious to leave to chance.
14. I find joy in my work and peace in my life when I am true to myself.
15. I am now the person I always wanted to be—the BEST of myself.

Bibliography

Carr, Allen, <u>Allen Carr's Easy Way to stop Smoking</u>, Prospero Books, a division of Chapters Inc. Finland. Held in Canada, 1997.

Gebhardt, Jack, <u>The Enlightened Smoker's Guide to quitting</u>, Element Book Inc. Founder of the smoker's freedom school, Australia, 1998.

Golden, Edwin R., <u>Welcome to the Unhooked Celebration: How to Stop Smoking and Start Living</u>, Dorrance Publishing Co. Pittsburgh, Pennsylvania, 1992.

Grant Viagas, Belinda, <u>Just Quit: Giving Up Smoking the Holistic Way,</u> Fusion Press, London, 2000.

Shapiro, Susan, <u>Lighting up: How I stopped Smoking, Drinking and everything else I loved except Sex</u>, Bantam Dell, New York, 2005.

Websites

There are thousands and thousands of websites on quitting smoking. Just go online and search: quitting smoking—or tips for stopping smoking—methods or best ways to stop smoking. Here is a list of the most important ones:

American Lung Association
www.lungusa.org
Canadian Lung Association
www.on.lungs.ca/nosmoking/tips.html
American Diabetes Association
www.diabetes.org
Canadian Cancer Society. Lung Cancer
www.cancer.ca
BC HEALTH Files #91—Quitting smoking—ministry of Health
www.bchealthguide.org/healthfiles/hfile91

Hypnosis and Hypnotherapy—FAQ
www.self-mastery.net/faq.htm

National Center for Chronic Disease Prevention—you can quit smoking
www.cdc.gov/tobacco/quit/canquit.htm

Nicotine Anonymous—One Day at a time
www.nicotine-anonymous.org/

Release for Life
http://releaseforlife.com

Tobacco Free. org—Motivating youth to stay tobacco free. Empowering smokers to quit
www.tobaccofree.org/quitting.htm

Smoking and Heart Disease
www.webmd.com

www.ingramcontent.com/pod-product-compliance
Lightning Source LLC
Chambersburg PA
CBHW031633160426
43196CB00006B/399